Teacher's
Resource
Book 3

NELSON ENGLISH

John Jackman and Wendy Wren

Contents

3 Introduction to Nelson English

5 Introduction to Skills Book 3 and Development Book 3

Curriculum Correlation charts:

6 National Curriculum (1995) England and Wales

8 Scottish Guidelines English Language 5 – 14

10 Northern Ireland English Curriculum Orders

Nelson English Skills Track Scope and Sequence charts:

12 Grammar and Punctuation

14 Spelling

16 Vocabulary

Nelson English Development Track Scope and Sequence chart:

18 Introduction

19 Development chart

Skills Book 3:

23 Scope and Sequence chart

Teaching Notes and Photocopy Masters (pcms):

25 Unit 1: Winter weather

28 Unit 2: Be your own weather forecaster

31 Unit 3: King James

34 Unit 4: Tudor and Stuart pastimes

37 Unit 5: Wings

40 Unit 6: The Ganges – a holy river

43 Unit 7: How Mowgli joined the wolves

45 Unit 8: Fire beneath our feet

48 Unit 9: Fire!

51 Unit 10: Victorian homes

53 Unit 10a: Victorian fashion

56 Unit 11: Travelling the River Amazon

59 Unit 11a: Caves and underground rivers

62 Unit 12: Fascinating body facts

64 Unit 13: Newspapers

67 Unit 14: Moon – in the future

72 Unit 14a: Earth

75 Check-up Answers

Development Book 3:

78 Scope and Sequence chart

Teaching Notes and Photocopy Masters (pcms):

79 Unit 1: A Winter's tale

81 Unit 2: Footprints in the snow

83 Unit 3: Tudor and Stuart theatre

85 Unit 4: Tudor and Stuart beliefs

87 Unit 5: Gale warning!

89 Unit 6: India

91 Unit 7: An Indian childhood

93 Unit 8: Remember, remember...

95 Unit 9: Bushfire

96 Unit 10: Victorian schooldays

98 Unit 11: Forests

100 Unit 12: Eat to live

101 Unit 13: Printing and writing

103 Unit 13a: Read all about it!

105 Unit 14: Earth...In the beginning

107 Quiz answers

Record of Progress charts:

108 Skills Book 3

109 Development Book 3

110 Acknowledgements

Nelson

Nelson English Components

UK Curriculum Coverage

Age range	Skills track	Development track	Teacher's resource books	NC Level	5–14 Level	NIC Level
Foundation 5-7 years				1/2	A/B	1/2
Book 1 7-8 years				3	B	3
Book 2 8-9 years				3/4	B/C	3/4
Book 3 9-10 years				4	C	4
Book 4 10-11 years				4/5	D	4/5
Book 5 11-12 years				5	D/E	5

Introduction to Nelson English

What is Nelson English?
Nelson English is a twin-track course which aims to provide an underpinning structure to the teaching of English for key stages 1 and 2 (England, Wales and Northern Ireland) and levels A–D/E (Scotland), focusing particularly on the knowledge, skills and understanding of writing. Throughout the course reading, listening and speaking opportunities are built in at all levels. **Nelson English (NE)** is also suitable for those older pupils who need more support.

The basic skills (including punctuation, grammar, spelling etc.) are mainly tackled within the **Skills** track while the conceptual skills relating to the craft of writing are the stuff of the **Development** track. In the **Skills** track the material tends to be more skills focused but still within a context. In the **Development** track the material tends to be more developmental or meaning based, but again, not without skills. You simply can't have one without the other.

Nelson English recognises the richness and range of good practice in most schools, and provides a systematic progression to enable young writers to acquire and develop the skills necessary to realise their full potential.

Any craft, including good functional, personal and imaginative writing, requires key skills and knowledge. Whilst recognising that there are many different approaches and attitudes to the teaching of English, **NE** provides teaching materials that can offer a graded progression to the acquisition of basic skills and understanding of language.

Nelson English seeks, unambiguously, to help to teach the skills of English and to provide the young writer with the 'tools of the trade'. These go beyond simply covering the predictable rules of punctuation, grammar, spelling, vocabulary etc., important as these are. The course also identifies as skills those strategies which are required to 'convey meaning in written language matching style to audience and purpose'. (*English in the National Curriculum*, Attainment target 3: Writing, page 12.) **NE** addresses these concepts, supplying learning opportunities to facilitate well-constructed plot, character creation, and so on. By using throughout a wide range of carefully selected stimulus material, the course provides opportunities to work in the full range of genres appropriate to the children's interests, and complementary to other curriculum requirements.

What does Nelson English comprise?
Nelson English begins at **Foundation Level** with a **Skills Big Book** supported by three **Skills Workbooks** and a **pupils' book**. (The workbook material is also available as copymasters in the **Teacher's Resource Book**.) The parallel **Development** track comprises a **pupils' book** which ties in with the **Skills** track materials or can stand alone if required.

The **Foundation Level** is followed by five further levels, each comprising a **pupils' book** in each track. The **pupils' books** contain a number of teaching units: most units are four or six pages in extent, and each might be expected to provide the English work for an average child for about a week. The material is so sequenced that the units from the two tracks complement each other, and may be used together – either with the whole class, with groups or with individual children. However the tracks are carefully devised to stand alone if required.

All English teaching requires a context, and **NE** has focused on the themes which research in many schools has indicated are consistently used by many teachers. These themes provide a purposeful context in both tracks on which the underpinning English work is built. Pupils will perhaps have had previous exposure to the themes used, will currently be working on them, or this course will serve as an introduction to forthcoming work in other curricular areas. But whatever the circumstances in each particular classroom, the context is essentially secondary to the core English teaching for which the books are designed.

The pupils' material is supported and extended by a **Teacher's Resource Book** at each level. These books contain extensive photocopiable material devised to help children who need additional support and consolidation. Some of these photocopy masters also provide extension activities. These books give the answers to the **pupils' book** exercises where appropriate.

How should Nelson English be used?
Different schools will have different approaches, so methods of usage will differ, but the course has been planned from the outset for maximum flexibility of use.

- Providing the 'essential diet', **NE** can be used as a comprehensive, stand-alone English course.
- The tracks can be used in parallel, with pupils in a class working on complementary units across both tracks. Alternatively, the tracks may be followed sequentially or even independently from each other.
- Many schools will want their pupils to work through much of **NE** independently and at their own pace, but the books are written assuming a degree of teacher intervention and support if the most effective use is to be made of the ideas and material offered. Attention to page design at an early stage has resulted in an accessible and inviting layout to children.
- As a rich resource, **NE** might be dipped into, to reinforce the work of the whole class or individuals as required.
- As a complement to cross-curricular topic work, **NE** will deepen and extend the opportunities for language work.
- At **Foundation Level**, the school may elect either to adopt the **Workbooks** to support the skills introduced in the **Skills Big Book**, or teachers may opt to photocopy this material from the accompanying **Teacher's Resource Book**.

Teachers who choose to use **NE** as a dip-in resource or to use the **Development** track alone, are advised that certain required skills are introduced in the **Skills** track, such as the use of a dictionary in **Skills Book 2**. For this reason teachers not using the **Skills** track, or who are working through **NE** in their own order, will need to teach these skills to enable their pupils to tackle confidently some of the work given in the **Development** track.

How is Nelson English assessed?

Assessment and record keeping provision is an important component of the materials. Frequent revision and testing of the skills in the pupils' books is supported by copiable records of pupils' progress. These provide opportunities for teachers to constantly, but conveniently, monitor and estimate progress and attainment. There is a simple but comprehensive record sheet for each book, so there are two sheets at each level.

The record sheets (see pages 108 – 109) may be produced in duplicate as it can be a positive incentive for the children to complete their own copies as they tackle the activities in **Nelson English**.

Teachers may choose to make work storage folders from their own more elaborately completed record sheets, enabling them to keep selected samples of work from exercises in the **Development** track, together with the sheets of paper on which the **Skills** track *Check-ups* were undertaken. This simple strategy conveniently provides the necessary profiling evidence required to demonstrate understanding and progress in the skills and concepts learnt as the child progresses through the carefully graded course.

During the development of this course, some schools experimented with pupil self-assessment, and this has been found a useful activity in a number of cases. Some teachers constructed simple questionnaires for their pupils to answer at various stages. It is important, however, that self-assessment by pupils of this age should always be a positive activity, steering them to indicate what has been enjoyed and where success has been realised, rather than where failure has been experienced. Suitably worded leading questions, in which children might admit to a lower 'enjoyment rating', can often lead the alert teacher to realise that the lack of enjoyment in undertaking a particular task might well be the result of lack of understanding. We have not, therefore, provided specific self-assessment sheets, but the record sheets have been designed to enable pupils to use them too, if so desired.

How does Nelson English relate to the statutory national curricula?

As is clear from the correlation charts and scope and sequence charts which appear on the following pages, **Nelson English** has been produced to meet the essential requirements of the curricula currently in use throughout the United Kingdom. Where these requirements differ the material errs in favour of introducing skills or concepts sooner rather than later. In order to ensure adequate consolidation prior to assessment, the teaching of most skills and concepts is introduced, at an appropriate level of understanding, as early as possible.

Nelson English is a *core* English course and minor modifications to the curricula documents are unlikely to require adjustments to the basic programme.

How is the work in Nelson English sequenced?

As with course materials in other subjects, such as mathematics, new skills and concepts are introduced slowly and progressively. Starting with a firm foundation of the requirements for the youngest age groups, the material in all its facets is progressive and repetitive. It is never assumed that a concept has been mastered or internalised simply because it has been introduced before. Opportunities are constantly offered for reinforcement and revision, and when related skills and concepts are being introduced the activities are designed to allow for the earlier material to be revisited.

However, **Nelson English** seeks neither to over-estimate the potential of the young writer, nor to be condescending. Whilst being careful to present material at a stage and in a manner accessible to the majority of pupils, the authors believe that within their individual limitations most children prefer to be tested and stretched.

The Scope and Sequence charts which appear on pages 12 – 17, 19 – 22, 23 and 77 summarise the content of the whole course in general and the content of the two Books Three in detail, and illustrate where a skill or concept is initially introduced and where and how frequently it is returned to in the pupils' books.

Where and when to introduce new skills and concepts has been carefully planned. Draft materials have been tested with the project trial schools, some of which integrated the framework into their curriculum plans whilst the project was still in preparation, which has benefited the programme.

Local knowledge and the experience of teachers will quite properly suggest different regimes for approaching the teaching of English, both from child to child and from school to school. Also much will depend on the style and approach of English teaching to which a child has previously been exposed. Evidence has shown that children who have not been accustomed or expected to apply themselves to more structured English tasks are soon able and happy to apply themselves productively to this type of work, alongside the equally important freer language work which exists in all good classrooms.

The structure and sequencing of **Nelson English** is intended to *support* not *supplant* existing good practice.

Introduction to Skills Book 3 and Development Book 3

Many children coming to these books will have had exposure to the **Foundation Level** and/or the books at **Level 1** of the **Nelson English** course. For these children some of the concepts and skills taught in the earlier part of the books will provide on-going practice and consolidation.

For other children these two books will be their first encounter with structured language work of this sort, so not only will the content be new to them, but the method of working will also require careful introduction. However experience has shown that most children enjoy, and soon get considerable satisfaction from, progressing through such a course.

Teachers will use their own experience to determine whether or when to arrange for some of the work to be conducted in groups. Generally, at the specific request of teachers who helped with the development of this course, the material assumes children will be working individually and independently. Opportunities for oral work are therefore usually pointed out in the notes addressed to the teacher rather than in the instructions contained within the **pupils' books**. Comprehension passages and questions may be introduced orally before they are tackled in writing. Occasionally they may be purely oral. Throughout the Development Books there is a system of bulleted stimulus questions. Again, these should encourage discussion and thought and are not necessarily intended to be answered either literally or in writing.

The teaching notes also draw attention to changes in the paragraph styles found in **NE**. Original text has a fully blocked first paragraph followed by indented paragraphs, but quoted material retains its original paragraph style. This is most noticeable in the **Development** track, where extracts from traditional and modern fiction are frequently used. These variations in style provide an opportunity for encouraging children to think about the presentation of English and the reasons for these conventions of style, and to share their ideas with the group or class.

The various teaching approaches and methodologies adopted in these books will not be new to most teachers. To ensure variety and maximise interest levels, often more than one teaching approach may be adopted, as in the spelling sections.

The comprehension has an emphasis on the literal in the **Skills** track, where it is intended above all to train the child to read the text, or to look carefully at the pictures for understanding and information. Inferential comprehension is introduced, mainly in the **Development** track, so that children can begin to 'read between the lines', and form opinions about what they read. Teachers are encouraged to develop children's listening and speaking skills by trying the comprehension orally, and by asking the children to make up their own cloze and comprehension activities for each other. It is important that children read widely on subjects that are of interest to them, so individual or group research efforts using class reference books or other material should be facilitated. **NE** is planned to discourage simple copying and encourage children to read – with accuracy – the lines, between the lines and beyond the lines. The intention is to enthuse children about English and, to this end, it should also be noted that the cloze questions, which throughout **Skills Book 3** precede those requiring sentence answers, are deliberately simple. The intention is that virtually all the children in the class will be able to complete the A section of the comprehension.

The vocabulary and grammar sections in **Skills Book 3** introduce concepts in line with the curriculum documents, but also take account of teachers' expectations. The punctuation exercises and activities are gently graded and sometimes repetitive in recognition of the need to provide regular reinforcement.

Whilst **NE** is not a comprehensive spelling programme, nevertheless it includes, through a combination of approaches, visual and aural activities to teach or reinforce the main spelling patterns, exercises covering notorious difficulties and teaching of the main rules.

As with earlier books, **Development Book 3** continues to give children a wide variety of stimulus material. The written work is a consolidation from earlier books leading onto more varied and demanding writing tasks.

The elements of narrative writing introduced in **Development Book 2** are now drawn together and children are required to consider plot, character and setting at the planning stage. **Development Book 3** leads them to analyse story beginnings and endings, and to consider feelings as well as physical descriptions when dealing with characters.

Factual writing is analysed more closely in terms of fact and opinion, leading to interpreting events in the form of newspaper reports and eye-witness accounts. The children are introduced to persuasive and dissuasive writing through the form of travel brochures.

Work on play scripts is introduced as are personal and autobiographical writing, interviews and more sophisticated research skills.

There is more emphasis on purpose and audience as children of this age can more readily understand that the style of a piece of writing is closely connected to the purpose for which it is written. Various treatments of similar themes are examined and children are asked to write for specific audiences.

Clearly **Skills Book 3** and **Development Book 3** are designed to allow individual and independent work, but teachers will recognise both those pupils who will from time to time benefit from more support, and where on occasions some activities might benefit from collaborative endeavour.

Nelson English Skills Book 3 Curriculum Correlation

Nelson English and the National Curriculum (1995) England and Wales

Programme of Study / Context	1 Winter weather	2 Be your own weather forecaster	3 King James	4 Tudor and Stuart pastimes	5 Wings	6 The Ganges – a holy river	7 How Mowgli joined the wolves	8 Fire beneath our feet	9 Fire!	10 Victorian homes	10a Victorian fashion	11 Travelling the River Amazon	11a Caves and underground rivers	12 Fascinating body facts	13 Newspapers	14 Moon – in the future	14a Earth
Developing compositional skills																	
Wide-ranging vocabulary																	
enrichment	5	9	14	17, 19	23, 25	28, 29	31, 33	35, 36	41	45	50, 51	54	58	64, 65	68, 69	72, 73	75, 77
encouraging choices		9, 10		17				36							68	72, 73	
Structuring grammatically/ coherently																	
nouns				18						40							75
pronouns		11		18													
singular/plural	7						37						58, 59				
verbs							32, 33			46			58, 59	65		72	76
tenses			14				32, 33			46						72	
adjectives/adverbs	7				28	33						54	58	64			76
conjunctions				24							50						
Developing presentational skills																	
Punctuation																	
capital letters								36, 37							68		
full stops				24				36, 37							68		
question marks				24				36							68		
exclamation marks								36							68		
commas		10	14	24				36							68		
direct speech	6			24	28, 29			36				55			68		
apostrophes				24	28, 29			36, 37	40			55			68		
paragraphs									40								
personal letters						32										70	
Spelling																	
dictionary/thesaurus	7														68	71	76
regular patterns		11	14	19	25	29	33	37	41	47	51	55	59	65	68, 69	73	77
silent letters			15														
word families									41		50	55	59				
same sounds	5																77
prefix/suffix			13						39	47	51	55	59				
Developing reading skills																	
wide range	4	8	12	16, 17	22	26, 27	30	34	38	44	48, 49	52, 53	56, 57	62, 63	66, 67	70	75
understanding	4	8, 9	12, 13	16, 17	22, 23	26, 27	30, 31	34, 35	38, 39	44, 45	48, 49	52, 53	56, 57	62, 63	66, 67	70, 71	74, 75

Nelson English Development Book 3 Curriculum Correlation

Nelson English and the National Curriculum (1995) England and Wales

Programme of Study / Context	1 A Winter's tale	2 Footprints in the snow	3 Tudor and Stuart theatre	4 Tudor and Stuart beliefs	5 Gale warning!	6 India	7 An Indian childhood	8 Remember, remember...	9 Bushfire	10 Victorian schooldays	11 Forests	12 Eat to live	13 Printing and writing	13a Read all about it!	14 Earth... In the beginning
Using different forms for different purposes															
Functional writing, incl. purpose/audience/ planning/forms		11 - 13		26, 27	32 - 35		44, 45		53	62, 63	67	69 - 71	74, 75	80	
Personal writing, incl. purpose/audience/ sequencing/depicting emotion/forms				28		38 - 40			56	62, 63		75			
Imaginative writing, incl. drafting/plot, setting, dialogue, character/poetry	5 - 9		16 - 19	21, 22			43	48 - 51		62, 63	65		75		
Using a wide-ranging vocabulary	9	13	19	23	29	35	41	45	51	57	63	67	71	75	80
Developing reading skills															
wide range	7, 8	10, 12	14 - 18	20, 21, 23	24 - 27	30, 32 - 34	36, 37	42 - 44	46 - 48	52, 54 - 55	58, 62	64, 66	68	72 - 74	76 - 78
understanding	4	10 - 13	14, 15	20	24, 25	30, 31	36, 37	42	46, 47	52 - 55	58 - 61	64 - 66	68, 69	72, 73	76 - 79

Nelson English Skills Book 3 Curriculum Correlation

Nelson English and the Scottish Guidelines English Language 5–14

Programme of Study Context	1 Winter weather	2 Be your own weather forecaster	3 King James	4 Tudor and Stuart pastimes	5 Wings	6 The Ganges – a holy river	7 How Mowgli joined the wolves	8 Fire beneath our feet	9 Fire!	10 Victorian homes	10a Victorian fashion	11 Travelling the River Amazon	11a Caves and underground rivers	12 Fascinating body facts	13 Newspapers	14 Moon – in the future	14a Earth
Punctuation and structure:																	
capital letters							36, 37							68			
full stops					24		36, 37							68			
question marks					24		36							68			
commas		10	14		24		36							68			
exclamation marks							36							68			
direct speech	6				24	28, 29	36				55			68			
Spelling:																	
graduated spelling		11	14	19	25	29	33	37	41	47	51	55	59	65	68, 69	73	77
spelling rules	7				28, 29				47	51		59				77	
alphabet/dictionary and thesaurus	7													68	71	76	
Knowledge about language:																	
nouns				18					40							75	
plurals	7						37					58, 59					
verbs						32, 33		46				58, 59	65		72	76	
adjectives/adverbs	7				28	33					54	58	64			76	
connectives				24					50								
tenses		14			32, 33		46							72			
pronouns		11		18													
paragraphs								40									
sentences				24		36, 37								68			

Nelson English Development Book 3 Curriculum Correlation

Nelson English and the Scottish Guidelines English Language 5–14

Programme of Study Context	1 A Winter's tale	2 Footprints in the snow	3 Tudor and Stuart theatre	4 Tudor and Stuart beliefs	5 Gale warning!	6 India	7 An Indian childhood	8 Remember, remember...	9 Bushfire	10 Victorian schooldays	11 Forests	12 Eat to live	13 Printing and writing	13a Read all about it!	14 Earth... In the beginning
Functional writing, incl. purpose/audience/ planning/forms		11–13			26, 27	32–35		44, 45		53	62, 63	67	69–71	74, 75	80
Personal writing, incl. purpose/audience/ sequencing/depicting emotion/forms					28		38–40			56	62, 63			75	
Imaginative writing, incl. drafting/plot, setting, dialogue, character/ poetry	5–9		16–19	21, 22				43	48–51		62, 63	65		75	
Vocabulary (appropriate/varied)	9	13	19	23	29	35	41	45	51	57	63	67	71	75	80
Reading comprehension (literal/inferential)	4	10–13	14, 15	20	24, 25	30, 31	36, 37	42	46, 47	52–55	58–61	64–66	68, 69	72, 73	76–79

Nelson English Skills Book 3 Curriculum Correlation

Nelson English and the Northern Ireland English Curriculum Orders

Programme of Study / Context	1 Winter weather	2 Be your own weather forecaster	3 King James	4 Tudor and Stuart pastimes	5 Wings	6 The Ganges – a holy river	7 How Mowgli joined the wolves	8 Fire beneath our feet	9 Fire!	10 Victorian homes	10a Victorian fashion	11 Travelling the River Amazon	11a Caves and underground rivers	12 Fascinating body facts	13 Newspapers	14 Moon – in the future	14a Earth
Acquisition of vocabulary:	5	9, 10	14	17, 19	23, 25	28, 29	31, 33	35, 36	41	45	50, 51	54	58	64, 65	68, 69	72, 73	75, 77
Grammatical conventions and Standard English:																	
nouns				18						40							
plurals	7						37						58, 59				
verbs							32, 33			46			58, 59	65		72	76
adjectives/adverbs	7				28		33					54	58	64			76
conjunctions						24					50						
tenses			14				32, 33			46						72	
pronouns		11		18													
Conventions of punctuation:																	
capital letters								36, 37							68		
full stops						24		36, 37							68		
question marks						24		36							68		
commas		10	14			24		36							68		
apostrophes						24	28, 29	36, 37	40			55			68		
personal letters							32									70	
exclamation marks								36							68		
direct speech	6					24	28, 29	36				55			68		
paragraphs									40								
Conventions of orthography:																	
common patterns		11	14	19	25	29	33	37	41	47	51	55	59	65	68, 69	73	77
dictionary/thesaurus	7														68	71	76

Nelson English Development Book 3 Curriculum Correlation

Nelson English and the Northern Ireland English Curriculum Orders

Programme of Study Context	1 A Winter's tale	2 Footprints in the snow	3 Tudor and Stuart theatre	4 Tudor and Stuart beliefs	5 Gale warning!	6 India	7 An Indian childhood	8 Remember, remember…	9 Bushfire	10 Victorian schooldays	11 Forests	12 Eat to live	13 Printing and writing	13a Read all about it!	14 Earth… In the beginning
Writing for a purpose and readership	6, 9	13	18, 19	22	26-28	34, 35	38-40	44, 45	48-51	53, 56		65, 67	69-71	74, 75	80
Planning the writing	5-9	13	16, 17	21, 22	26-28	32, 33	38-40	44, 45	48-51	53, 56	62, 63	65, 67	69-71	73	80
Acquisition of vocabulary	9	13	19	23	29	35	41	45	51	57	63	67	71	75	80
Reading comprehension	4	10-13	14, 15	20	24, 25	30, 31	36, 37	42	46, 47	52-55	58-61	64-66	68, 69	72, 73	76-79

11

Nelson English Skills Book 3

Numbers refer to pages in Skills Book 3
- see relevant Teacher's Resource Book for details.

Scope and Sequence: Grammar and Punctuation

	F	Bk1	Bk2	Bk3	Bk4	Bk5
abbreviations			•			•
addresses		•		32		•
adjectives	•	•	•	7/28/33/64	•	
adjectives/possessive						•
adverbs			•	76	•	
apostrophe		•	•		•	
article						•
capitals	•	•	•	37	•	•
clauses					•	•
colon						•
commas		•	•	10/14	•	•
comparative	•	•	•	54/64	•	
contractions		•	•		•	•
conjunctions	•	•		24/50/51	•	
consonants	•	•				
direct speech			•	6/28/36/55	•	•
editing				68		
exclamation marks			•		•	•
full stops	•	•	•	24/36/68	•	•
hyphens					•	
indirect speech				6		•
inverted commas			•	6/28/36/55	•	•
letter writing				32	•	•
negatives					•	
nouns/abstract					•	•
nouns/collective	•		•	18	•	
nouns/common	•	•			•	
nouns/proper	•	•			•	
paragraphs			•	40		•
'parts of speech'						•
phrases		•			•	•
plural	•	•	•	7/37	•	
possessive nouns			•	40		
predicate			•	18		•

	F	Bk1	Bk2	Bk3	Bk4	Bk5
prepositions	•				•	
pronouns				11	•	•
pronouns/possessive					•	•
pronouns/relative						•
punctuation	•	•	•	24/36/68	•	•
question marks	•	•	•	24/36	•	•
sentences/simple	•	•	•	24		•
sentences/compound				24		•
singular	•	•	•			
spoken English					•	
subject			•	18		
superlative	•	•	•	58/64	•	
syllables				76		•
titles	•				•	
verbs	•	•	•			•
verbs/active: passive					•	•
verbs/agreement				58/59	•	
verbs/auxiliary			•	65/72	•	•
verbs/tense				14/32/46/72	•	
vowels	•	•	•			
words	•					

Nelson English Skills Book 3

Numbers refer to pages in Skills Book 3
• see relevant Teacher's Resource Book for details.

Whilst many of the spelling patterns will be introduced by teachers in the context of the work in the Foundation Level, systematic teaching of the spelling patterns begins in Skills Book 1.

Scope and Sequence: Spelling

Pattern	F	Bk1	Bk2	Bk3	Bk4	Bk5	Examples
alphabet	•	•	•	7			
initial letters	•						
short vowels	•						cat/log
ch	•		•				chip
sh	•	•	•				shop
th		•					thin
ar		•					car
ck		•					sack
oo		•					book/food
ee		•					bee
ea		•	•				sea/head
ow		•					cow/crow
ou		•					mouse
a–e		•					game
i–e		•					kite
o–e		•					rope
u–e		•					use
ing/double cons't.		•			•	•	sitting
ing/drop e		•				•	making
ear		•		19			hear
wa		•					was
making plurals		•	•	7/37	•	•	
soft c		•		25			face
er			•				letter
ir			•				bird
ur			•				nurse
o as /u/			•				mother
ai			•				nail
ay			•				play
or			•				fork
igh			•				high
ew			•				few
oy			•				toy
oi			•				boil
aw			•				fawn
oa			•				boat
silent letters			•	15	•		knife/write
ough			•				thought
ed suffix				14/32/46	•		jumped
le/el/al				69			table/travel/hospital

Pattern	F	Bk1	Bk2	Bk3	Bk4	Bk5	Examples
tch				11			catch
'i before e'				29			chief
dge endings				77			bridge
age endings				65			message
tion endings				55			station
able endings				47	•		enjoyable
ible endings				51	•		possible
ure endings				33			picture
are				41			care
ness suffix				59			darkness
ght endings				73			sight
sure endings					•		measure
augh					•		caught
ckle					•		pickle
ssion					•		confession
l or ll					•		skilful
French derivations					•		campaign
ance/ence					•		entrance silence
gue endings					•		catalogue
ous/ious					•	•	generous/ delicious
ery/ary						•	slippery/ missionary
'e' ending and suffixes						•	waking/ wakeful
'y' ending and suffixes						•	ugly/ ugliness
adding prefixes						•	dissatisfy

Nelson English Skills Book 3

Numbers refer to pages in Skills Book 3
• see relevant Teacher's Resource Book for details.

Scope and Sequence: Vocabulary

	F	Bk1	Bk2	Bk3	Bk4	Bk5
abbreviations			•			•
acronyms						•
alliteration				68		•
alphabetical order	•	•	•	7		
anagrams					•	
antonyms	•		•	23/71		•
borrowed words			•		•	
changing words						•
classifying	•	•	•			
codes		•	•	19		
collective nouns			•	18		•
comparatives	•	•	•	54/64	•	
compound words		•	•	5	•	
confusing words		•	•	45	•	
contractions		•	•		•	
conversation words						•
days	•	•				
definitions		•	•		•	•
dialect					•	
dictionary	•	•	•		•	•
eponyms						•
foreign words					•	
gender words			•	75		•
glossary			•	12		
glyphs			•			
homonyms			•		•	
homophones			•	5/77	•	•
hyperbole					•	
hyphenated words					•	
idioms					•	•
interjections					•	
metaphors						•
months	•	•				
number words	•				•	
onomatopoeia				9	•	•
over-worked words				10/17/73	•	
palindromes				51		
plurals	•		•	7/37	•	
prefixes			•	13/39	•	•
proverbs					•	
puns						•
question words	•		•			
redundant words						•
repetition						•
rhyming words	•		•	25		
root words				50/59	•	
sign language				41		

	F	Bk1	Bk2	Bk3	Bk4	Bk5
similes			•	31		
spoonerisms					•	
suffixes			•	39	•	•
superlatives	•		•	58/64	•	
syllables				76		•
synonyms	•		•	36/68/71	•	•
thesaurus				71	•	•
word associations				15/35/65		
word families			•	50/59		
word webs						•
words within words			•	11	•	

Development Track Scope and Sequence

The units in each of the **Development Books** comprise the following:

Stimulus

The stimulus material within each book is varied to allow children to read and experience a wide range of genres including modern and traditional poetry; modern and long-established fiction; traditional tales, such as myths and legends; factual material in the forms of text, charts, diagrams, etc.; famous paintings and pictures.

It is left to the teacher's discretion as to how this stimulus material is introduced. It can be read, looked at and discussed by the class in groups, or children can tackle it individually.

Comprehension

Following each unit stimulus are comprehension questions. These are usually both literal – reading for understanding and information, and inferential – allowing children to engage with and respond to the stimulus. No specific writing instruction is given, to allow the teacher to use a variety of approaches – class discussion; group discussion/writing and reporting back; individual writing.

Some exercises request written sentences in response but it may sometimes be more appropriate to allow other kinds of answer to be offered, such as pictures or oral answers.

Writing

The writing tasks vary according to the aims of the unit. In some they are related in context to the stimulus material, but sometimes they are related directly to stimulus passages in terms of style, purpose and audience, so that the stimulus can be used by the children as a model for their own writing.

The writing tasks are progressive, in that each style of writing is made up of various elements. Each element is introduced in turn and children are given the opportunity to build up their competence before tackling the whole.

For example, in narrative writing, the elements of plot, timing, setting and characters are introduced in turn, allowing children to build the whole picture of what is meant by 'write a story'. There is then detailed work on story beginnings and endings, deeper characterisation, non-sequential plot, etc., to give the opportunity for more interesting and complex writing. Similarly, diaries are initially introduced as ways of keeping records, but progress from listing events to examining and recording thoughts, feelings and reactions. Also, note-taking is initially tackled through looking for and recording specific pieces of information, but it progresses to much more broadly-based research skills.

By the end of the course, children will have learnt the craft of writing in a progressive and discretely structured way. They will have an understanding of, and will have practised, story writing, imaginative writing, descriptions, writing from personal experience, discursive writing and factual writing in a range of forms.

A word about poetry writing.

Poetry is used extensively as stimulus material throughout **Nelson English** but there are few occasions on which the children are asked to write a poem. The authors believe that poetry writing is too important and too difficult a skill to be lightly included in most units. The best children's poetry comes from an interaction between teacher and pupil and it is for the teacher to decide when this important kind of writing is most appropriate, and for which children. Different children will be ready for different kinds of poetry writing at different times as they progress through the material. Poetry writing can be a substitute for many of the prose writing tasks, or may be added to a unit's work, but the teacher is in the best position to decide the suitability of doing this, and to decide which children will respond positively. This is why the prescriptive poetry writing in **Nelson English** goes little beyond acrostics and limericks.

Working with words

This section appears at the end of each unit and is designed to extend the pupils' vocabulary, stimulate their interest in language and concentrate on particular aspects of language which will improve their writing. Exercises range from looking at the derivation of words to finding more interesting and appropriate adjectives, adverbs, etc.

This vocabulary work is in the context of each unit, and hopefully has the added benefit of providing a little light relief!

Nelson English Development Books

Scope and Sequence

Foundation

Writing	Examples
Comprehension	literal, inferential, picture from a variety of stimuli
Sentences	completing and writing
Narrative	picture sequencing completing stories
Imaginative	imaginative situations
Descriptive	familiar situations e.g. making a den
Personal	record keeping of events in diary form expressing preferences
Factual	simple reference books
Poetry	limericks
Lists	familiar contexts e.g. food, school

Book 1

Writing	Examples
Comprehension	literal, inferential, picture from a variety of stimuli
Sentences	completing and writing
Narrative	picture stories, completing stories
Imaginative	unfamiliar things e.g. Chinese dragons, life as a Roman soldier
Descriptive	use of adjectives purpose and audience familiar scenes e.g. houses, shops building up descriptions of objects e.g. trees matching written description with pictures describing pictures/drawings
Personal	expressing preferences e.g. where to live, favourite seasons, etc. personal experience e.g. sounds at night, etc.
Factual	plans, instructions, rules analysing diagrams, maps research – simple reference books, dictionaries factual texts e.g. history
Poetry	acrostics
Letters	personal
Lists	specific pieces of information specific groups of words e.g. adjectives books/poems/stories on a given theme

Book 2

Writing	Examples
Comprehension	literal, inferential, picture from a variety of stimuli Emphasis on a) inferential – fictional texts; b) literal – reading for information – non-fiction
Sentences	completing – from given phrases e.g. time writing – based on research

Book 2 Continued

Writing	Examples
Narrative	completing stories more complex picture stories – story structure planning a story – plot, time, character, setting book covers – fiction
Imaginative	sequence of events in unfamiliar situations imaginative element in narrative writing imaginary places and objects e.g. vehicles, islands involvement in given situation e.g. Wright Brothers' first flight, Robin Hood adventure
Descriptive	building up descriptions of objects matching written descriptions with pictures descriptive element in narrative writing descriptions from photographs settings e.g. island feelings in a given context e.g. William Tell descriptions based on information in stimulus passage
Personal	expressing preference e.g. food, jobs personal experience e.g. train journeys record-keeping of events in diary form
Factual	step-by-step instructions e.g. making a sandwich recording information in the form of a graph, chart, map research – reference books for information research – dictionary work to clarify meaning of stimulus passage non-fiction books – covers, contents page, index research – encyclopedias note-taking – specific pieces of information
Diaries	recording facts from stimulus passage based on pictures
Letters	personal – in context of stimulus passage
Lists	specific groups of words e.g. adverbs for a specific purpose – food/drink for a party

Book 3

Writing	Examples
Comprehension	literal, inferential, picture from a variety of more complex stimuli
Narrative	planning a story – setting, character, plot story beginnings story endings characters – actions and feelings
Imaginative	putting themselves in characters' places
Descriptive	describing pictures e.g. 'No fire for the antelope' describing situations – storms descriptive element in story writing

Book 3 Continued

Writing	Example
Personal	personal preference e.g. modern classroom/Victorian classroom personal experience – facts and feelings e.g. first day at school autobiographies time line
Factual	instructions – analysis e.g. Fireworks Code recording information in the form of a graph, chart, map research – encyclopedias research – compiling fact file note-taking – specific topic e.g. Guy Fawkes diagrams – analysis fact and opinion factual reports from pictures e.g. weather interview newspaper reports
Letters	personal letters describing experience e.g. birthday
Lists	for description – adjectives for emotions
Poetry	acrostics
Persuasive	holiday brochures – purpose and audience for and against a given topic e.g. school uniform
Analysis	comparing/contrasting serious and comic treatment of given subject comparing/contrasting narrative/factual writing comparing/contrasting persuasive/factual writing styles of writing – purpose and audience simple/complex styles – purpose and audience
Plays	setting out playscript converting story into playscript

Book 4

Writing	Examples
Comprehension	literal, inferential, picture from a variety of stimuli Stimulus will be of a greater complexity and questions will lead pupils to analyse for purpose and audience
Sentences	beginning sentences – style use of present participles, conjunctions, etc.
Narrative	first person narratives full stories science fiction stories elements of adventure, suspense, etc.
Imaginative	imaginative element in narrative writing
Descriptive	atmospheric writing for specific response
Personal	journals – events and responses personal experience – series of events

Book 4 Continued

Writing	Example
Factual	newspaper reports autobiography book blurbs note-taking business letters research
Persuasive	pros and cons
Structuring writing	paragraphs drafting rewriting
Analysis	purpose and audience

Book 5

Writing	Examples
Comprehension	literal, inferential, picture from a variety of stimuli Stimulus will be of a greater complexity and questions will lead pupils to analyse for purpose and audience
Narrative	characters – characterisation through dialogue/actions ghost stories mystery stories third person narrative
Imaginative	writing which is purely imaginary compared with writing about real situations which the writer has never experienced
Descriptive	more detailed description concentrating on a more mature vocabulary
Personal	personal responses/preferences to poetry and various styles of writing
Factual	summary book reviews openings/endings for factual accounts use of non-prose devices e.g. charts, graphs for presenting information business letters advertising
Persuasive	discursive essays openings/endings
Structuring writing	headings sub-headings layout magazine articles
Analysis	purpose and audience intended reader response
Poetry	purpose and style use of poetic devices: alliteration, imagery, metaphor, etc.

Skills Book 3 Scope and Sequence

Unit	Stimulus	Comprehension	Vocabulary	Punctuation/ Grammar	Spelling	Quiz
1 Winter weather	modern poetry; illustrations	cloze; literal; inferential	homophones; compound words	direct and indirect speech; making adjectives	f/fe plurals	scrambled words; alphabetical ordering
2 Be your own weather forecaster	cloud photographs; factual writing; cartoons	cloze; literal; inferential	onomatopoeia; over-used words (*nice*)	commas; pronouns	*tch* pattern	making words
3 King James	portrait; historical description	cloze; literal; inferential	prefixes	commas; tenses (present and past)	silent letters	word associations; missing letters
4 Tudor and Stuart pastimes	Joseph Nash print; historical description; pictures	cloze; literal; inferential	over-used words (*got*)	collective nouns; subject and predicate	*ear* pattern	decoding messages
5 Wings	factual text; photographs; pictures	cloze; literal; inferential	word shapes; antonyms	punctuation marks; conjunctions; compound sentences	soft *c*	word puzzle
6 The Ganges – a holy river	factual text; photographs; pictures	cloze; literal; inferential	adjectives made from countries	direct speech	*i* before *e*	world rivers
7 How Mowgli joined the wolves	narrative text – classic children's fiction; pictures	cloze; literal; inferential	similes	letter writing; verbs/past tense	*ure* pattern	animal match – adjectives
8 Fire beneath our feet	factual text; photograph; diagram; picture	cloze; literal; inferential	synonyms	sentences; direct speech	plurals/words ending in *o*	punctuation puzzle
9 Fire!	photographs; factual text; pictures	cloze; literal; inferential	word origins; suffix (*ful*)	paragraphs; possessive nouns	*are* pattern	sign language
10 Victorian homes	factual text; photographs; illustrations	cloze; literal; inferential	*where, were, we're*	past tense	*able* pattern	jumbled words – word order
10a Victorian fashion	factual text; captioned pictures; picture sequence	cloze; literal; inferential	root words	conjunctions; *who* and *which*	*ible* pattern	palindromes
11 Travelling the River Amazon	short narrative; photographs; pictures	cloze; literal; inferential	comparatives	conversations	*tion* pattern	rhyme

Skills Book 3 **Scope and Sequence** continued

Unit	Stimulus	Comprehension	Vocabulary	Punctuation/ Grammar	Spelling	Quiz
11a **Caves and underground rivers**	diagrammatic cut-away; text and labels	cloze; literal; inferential	superlatives	plural verbs	*ness* suffix	word trees
12 **Fascinating body facts**	captioned illustrations	cloze; literal; inferential	irregular adjectives	auxiliary verbs	*age* pattern	word selection
13 **Newspapers**	graph; cartoon; pictures	cloze; literal; inferential	alliteration; synonyms	editing	*le*, *el* and *al* endings	word jokes
14 **Moon – in the future**	letter; photograph	cloze; literal; inferential	using a thesaurus	future tense	*ght* pattern	*said* words
14a **Earth**	modern poetry; pictures	cloze; literal; inferential	gender words; syllables	adverbs	*dge* pattern	homophones

Skills Unit 1

Skills Book Aims:

1. To practise common homophones.
2. To review compound words.
3. To introduce indirect speech.
4. To introduce adjectives derived from nouns.
5. To teach plurals of words ending with *f* and *fe*.
6. To practise words with the *ai* vowel digraph.

Marking suggestion
Teachers may choose to paste photocopies of the unit answers on to cards and store these in a simple box, so the children can check their own answers, as appropriate.

Each card should be clearly labelled with the book title and unit number and title, to enable the children to find and use the correct unit answers easily.

Winter weather

Teaching notes

Stimulus	modern poetry; illustrations	At any time of the year weather is a good starting point for spoken and written English, offering as it does direct experiences to the child. Not by chance is it the most common subject for verbal interchange! Make a class anthology of weather poems, and also make and illustrate an anthology suitable for presentation to a younger class.
Comprehension	cloze; literal; inferential	See general note in introduction, page 5.
Vocabulary	homophones (weather/whether); compound words	Learning about homophones is a subtle, and important, way to improve spelling ability. Some pairs of words may not be homophones in some dialects, such as *weather/whether* and *four/for*. An interesting starting point for a discussion on dialects. Children might be asked to write silly sentences for each of the groups of homophones in the box. In pairs, children might write the components of about ten compound words on cards in such a way as to devise a dominoes-type game. Having made the game ask the children to write clear, concise instructions.
Punctuation/ Grammar	direct and indirect speech; making adjectives	**Pcm 1** offers additional support, which might usefully be supplemented by comparable oral/written activities. One group might write a report of a simple dialogue in direct speech, whilst a second group does so in indirect speech form. When making adjectives from nouns, revise the rule for doubling the consonant – short word, short vowel, double the last letter.
Spelling	*f/fe* plurals	Plurals of *f* and *fe* endings. **Pcm 2** gives additional practice.
Quiz	scrambled words; alphabetical ordering	Point out that some letter groups may make more than one word.

Answers

Comprehension

A 1 Monday
  2 Thursday
  3 freeze
  4 snow

B 1 I think the weather became colder as the week went on.
  2 Tuesday was the windiest day.
  3 The cold on Friday was enough to freeze your tears.
  4 Boxing Day was on a Tuesday that year. (Logical deduction.)

Vocabulary – homophones

A weather and whether

B 1 see, sea
  2 hear, here
  3 for, four
  4 They're, their, there
  5 whether, weather

Vocabulary – compound words

A sunshine, thunderstorm, hailstorm, rainfall, snowfall, raindrop, snowdrop, snowball

Grammar – direct and indirect speech

A direct speech indirect speech
   2, 3, 6   1, 4, 5

Grammar – making adjectives

A 1 rainy
  2 misty
  3 windy
  4 snowy
  5 icy
  6 chilly
  7 sunny
  8 breezy

Spelling – plurals, *f* and *fe* endings

A half, halves
   thief, thieves
   leaf, leaves
   knife, knives
   wife, wives
   calf, calves
   loaf, loaves

Quiz – scrambled words

1 snail
  (nails and slain are options too)
2 jail
3 mail/Liam
4 rain
5 lair/liar/rail

Quiz – alphabetical order

1 cold, hot, ice, rain
2 drop, forecast, shine, thunder
3 water, weather, whether, wind

See also: **p.79**, **Development** notes. 25

Direct and indirect speech

Direct speech needs inverted commas (speech marks).

Indirect speech reports what was said, but does not use the actual words spoken.

A Read these sentences.
Write 'direct' or 'indirect' next to each one.

1 "What are you doing after school?" asked Ranjit.

2 He told me that he had to help his Dad.

3 "I'll come and help too," I said.

4 "Good" he said, "that will be fun."

5 Ranjit said he was sure his Dad would not mind.

6 Ranjit's Dad thanked me for helping.

B These sentences are in direct speech. Rewrite them as indirect speech. The first is done to help you.

1 "Why do you feel cross?" she asked.

She asked me why I felt so cross.

2 "I don't like big dogs," said Nicola.

3 "This is a very gentle one," promised Nasreen.

C Rewrite these sentences so that they are in direct speech, with inverted commas where needed.

1 Will said that he hated duck eggs.

2 Mum said he had never had one.

3 He replied that he didn't like their smell.

Unit 1

Nelson ENGLISH SKILLS BOOK 3 Pcm 2

name _____ date _____

> Be careful!
> *chief, belief, reef, dwarf* and *roof* do not follow the rule.

f and *fe* endings

To make plurals of words that end with **f** or **fe** we usually change the f or fe to **v** and add **es**

A word that ends in **ff** is made plural by adding **s**.

A Colour the box next to the word that is needed to complete each sentence. Write each word you choose in the sentence gap.

1 Cowboys spent much of their _____ moving cattle.

    lives ☐   lifes ☐   livfes ☐

2 They wore _____ to protect their faces from the dust.

    scarfs ☐   scarves ☐   scarfes ☐

3 The cattle were kept away from the _____ .

    cliffs ☐   clivies ☐   cliffes ☐

4 Young _____ needed special care.

    calfs ☐   calves ☐   calfes ☐

5 Tribal _____ usually allowed the herds to pass.

    chieves ☐   chiefs ☐   chiefves ☐

6 Sometimes _____ would attack the herds.

    wolves ☐   wolfs ☐   wolfes ☐

B Write the plural form of these words.

1	half	_____	9	life	_____
2	knife	_____	10	wife	_____
3	cuff	_____	11	scarf	_____
4	calf	_____	12	roof	_____
5	belief	_____	13	dwarf	_____
6	loaf	_____	14	staff	_____
7	shelf	_____	15	thief	_____
8	leaf	_____	16	reef	_____

Published by Thomas Nelson and Sons Ltd 1995   Nelson English © John Jackman and Wendy Wren 1995.

Skills Unit 2

Skills Book Aims:

1 To introduce onomatopoeia.
2 To suggest alternative words to *nice*.
3 To practise using commas in lists of nouns and between adjectives.
4 To introduce pronouns.
5 To practise the *tch* spelling pattern.

Be your own weather forecaster

Teaching notes

Stimulus	cloud photographs; factual writing; cartoons	Collect a range of suitable information books about weather. Children can quickly become quite effective short-term forecasters. Video-record television weather forecasts, to compare with actual observations and records of the weather over several days. How accurate were the TV forecasters? Maybe write and tell them how well they have performed!
Comprehension	cloze; literal; inferential	See general note in introduction, page 5.
Vocabulary	onomatopoeia; over-used words (*nice*)	**Pcm 1** provides additional activities on onomatopoeic words. Always a good starting point for poetry writing with selected groups. Children might copy a number of sentences which contain the word *nice* from the board, replacing it with either *stupid* or *silly*; amusing - and salutary!
Punctuation/ Grammar	commas; pronouns	The correct use of commas in making lists is not a difficult concept, although children often need reminding about correct usage with respect to adjectives. **Pcm 2** practises work on pronouns.
Spelling	*tch* pattern	Another spelling pattern which needs to be practised.
Quiz	making words	If the children enjoy this game, invite them to find in their dictionary another long word for the same activity. All disputed spellings should be resolved with reference to the dictionary. (Cf. p108.)

Answers

Comprehension

A 1 forecast
2 white/cumulus
3 grey
4 cirrus clouds

B 1 We should expect showers when cumulus clouds slowly spread and cover the sky.
2 Large drops of rain fall from a cumulonimbus cloud (in a thunderstorm) because the air inside these clouds moves upwards very fast so small drops of rain get sucked upwards and do not fall downwards.
3 If there has been a drought, farmers would be most pleased to see cumulonimbus clouds.
4 I would like to see cirrus clouds on the evening before a visit to the beach, because light, wispy clouds high in the sky usually indicate fine weather.

Vocabulary – onomatopoeia

A **wind:** sings, rustles, pings, pounds, hums, strums, twangs, whishes, bangs, mumbles, grumbles, rumbles, crashes.
rain: pings, pounds, tinkles, strums, whishes, sprinkles, splishes, bangs, mumbles, grumbles, rumbles, patters, crashes.

B Options include:
1 rustle, crackle, crunch
2 swish, whoosh, splash
3 clink, clank, clatter
4 boom, bang
5 bang, thud, thump, crunch
6 gurgle, coo, murmur, babble

Vocabulary – over-used words: *nice*

A Options include:
It was a **sunny** day. It was **good** to see the sun shining. I put on my **fantastic** new trainers. My uncle said he had bought some **tasty** chicken and we could go for a **delicious** barbecue with my **favourite** cousin Lisa and her **friendly** little baby brother.

Punctuation – commas

A 1 Snow, rain, hail and sleet all fall from clouds.
2 We took crisps, cakes, fruit and sandwiches on the picnic.
3 Matthew, Nazaar, Laith, Claire and Ben came to the party.
4 For my birthday I hope to get a rabbit, trainers and a computer game.
5 My nan asked me to buy potatoes, biscuits, cream, oranges, sugar and a packet of burgers.

B 1 It was a warm, sunny, pleasant day to be windsurfing.
2 The cold, biting, northerly wind cut into me.
3 Dark, threatening storm clouds gathered overhead.

Grammar – pronouns

A 1 he
2 it
3 they
4 she

Spelling – *tch* pattern

B 1 patch
2 hatch
3 pitch
4 stitch

Quiz – high scorer

There are 175 words that can be made from **cumulonimbus**: how many can you make?
(The children will achieve higher scores if they can use dictionaries for this activity and if plurals are allowed!)

See also: **p.81**, **Development** notes.

Nelson English — Skills Book 3, Unit 2, Pcm 1

name _____ date _____

Onomatopoeic words (or sound words)

Snap! Crackle! Pop! are the sounds *Kellogg's Rice Krispies* are supposed to make.

A In her poem about weather, this poet uses many onomatopoeic words. Underline them.

It sings
and rustles
and pings
and pounds
and tinkles
and strums
and twangs
and whishes
and sprinkles
and splishes
and bangs
and mumbles
and grumbles
and rumbles
and flashes
and crashes.

Aileen Fisher

B Make a list of words to describe as many sounds as you can think of that you might hear at a bonfire party.

C Think of ten words that describe some of the different sounds you might hear at a birthday party.

Published by Thomas Nelson and Sons Ltd 1995   Nelson English © John Jackman and Wendy Wren 1995.

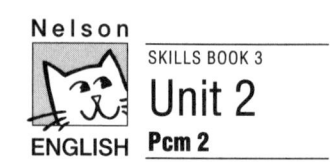

Pronouns

Remember that a **pronoun** takes the place of a noun.

A Choose a pronoun to replace the underlined nouns, then rewrite the sentences with the pronouns.

1 Mrs Lindsay is our teacher. Mrs Lindsay arranged a trip to the museum.
_____

2 The coach arrived. The coach would have room for everyone.
_____

3 Craig wanted to see the dinosaurs. Craig wanted to draw the dinosaurs.
_____

4 Our teacher asked Craig and Anna if Craig and Anna had finished.
_____

B Choose the correct pronoun from each pair.

1 _____ was wet (He/Him)
2 _____ was early (I/Me)
3 _____ was old (It/They)
4 between you and _____ (I/me)
5 _____ are good friends (We/Us)
6 _____ were tired (We/Us)
7 I like _____ (she/her)
8 the group of _____ (them/they)

C Some pronouns are used to show who or what owns someting. They are called **possessive** pronouns. Here are four possessive pronouns:

    hers   yours   mine   ours

Choose one of these pronouns for each of these gaps.

James found a packet of sweets.

"Are they _____ ?" asked Mrs Lindsay.

"No, they are _____ ," shouted Craig.

"But Anna says they are _____ ," said Ben.

"They can't be, they're _____ ," insisted the twins.

Skills Unit 3

Skills Book Aims:

1. To introduce prefixes, and practise *un*, *in*, *im* and *dis*.
2. To introduce the use of the comma to indicate a short pause.
3. To introduce the term *tense*, and practise present and past.
4. To practise 'silent letters'.
5. To develop the concept of word associations.

King James

Teaching notes

Stimulus	portrait; historical description	Historians have not all been kind to King James. Collect accounts from different sources to compare different versions and opinions.
Comprehension	cloze; literal; inferential	See general note in introduction, page 5.
Vocabulary	prefixes	**Pcm 1** practises prefixes which form the antonym (opposite).
Punctuation/ Grammar	commas; tenses (present and past)	**Pcm 2** gives further opportunities to explore the use of commas to aid meaning. **Pcm 3** extends the work on present and past tenses. Such work can be further developed by providing short passages relevant to current classroom interests, but which are required to be written in a different tense. Also provide a passage that requires editing due to its use of mixed tenses.
Spelling	silent letters	Make a class 'ghosts' picture, the idea being to illustrate as many words as possible which, like 'ghosts', have a silent letter. Draw ghost shapes around the silent letters.
Quiz	word associations; missing letters	These activities can each be followed by asking children to create similar exercises themselves for a friend or partner to undertake.

Answers

Comprehension

A 1 James
    2 killed
    3 thick, padded
    4 Guy Fawkes

B 1 His mother, Mary, Queen of Scots, left him in Scotland when she fled to England, and he learned that his father, Darnley, had been cruelly murdered.
    2 James wanted to increase taxes so that he could have more money to spend.
    3 Some people might have wanted to harm King James because he was not always careful enough about the decisions he reached, and some lords, priests and ordinary people were unhappy with his decisions.
    4 Some priests didn't want ordinary people to read the Bible because this meant that they would be able to challenge the priests' teachings.

Vocabulary – prefix

A 1 un(happy)
    2 dis(appear)
    3 un(tie)
    4 un(cover)/dis(cover)
    5 dis(trust)
    6 un(sure)
    7 in(capable)
    8 im(perfect)

Punctuation – commas

A 1 In spite of careful planning, Guy Fawkes and his friends were caught.
    2 King James was a very nervous person, always wearing padded clothes in case he was stabbed.
    3 The dark cellar, which was under the Houses of Parliament, was filled with gunpowder.
    4 Even the padded clothes, which were supposed to stop gun shots and stabbings, would not have saved King James from an explosion.

Grammar – present and past tense

A 1 I walked to school.
    2 Gill delivered the papers.
    3 We played football.
    4 We celebrated the festival.

B   hopped
      jumping
      helped
      cleaned
      sailed
      painting

Spelling – silent letters

(k)not (w)ren (g)naw
(k)now lam(b)
(w)reck (w)rite

Quiz – word associations

2 man
3 flowers
4 foot
5 composition/music
6 school
7 water/sea/ocean/river/lake
8 hand

Quiz – missing letters

1 k
2 tt
3 y

See also: **p.83**, **Development** notes.

Nelson English — Skills Book 3, Unit 3, Pcm 1

name _____ date _____

Prefixes which make antonyms (opposites)

A Underline the word in each of these sentences which has a prefix meaning *not*. Then draw a neat circle round the prefix in that word.

1 Julie found it impossible to sleep.

2 She disliked going to bed when it was still light.

3 Julie wondered whether all children felt unhappy about going to bed early.

4 Unfortunately, she had no choice, so she went to sleep.

B All of these words can be made to mean the opposite by adding *dis* or *un*. Write the antonym of each word.

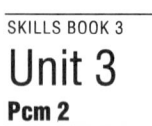

1 like _____
2 allow _____
3 dress _____
4 fair _____
5 healthy _____
6 even _____
7 pack _____
8 employed _____
9 qualify _____
10 trust _____

Nelson English — Skills Book 3, Unit 3, Pcm 2

name _____ date _____

Commas

Add commas where they are needed in these sentences.

1 The heavy rain caused flooding in Ipswich Maldon Harlow and Ongar.

2 The water washed away bridges roads and railway lines.

3 We spent the night bailing mopping clearing and worrying.

4 The mess and smell were terrible but we all helped each other clear up.

Published by Thomas Nelson and Sons Ltd 1995

Nelson English © John Jackman and Wendy Wren 1995.

Past tense

A Next to each of these sentences write **present** or **past** to show whether they are happening now (*present* tense) or whether they happened in the past (*past* tense).

1 The team played well yesterday. _____

2 I like eating ice-cream. _____

3 Mum is painting the hall. _____

4 The tent leaked and made us wet. _____

5 I am waiting for my friend. _____

B Write the past tense of these verbs.

1 jump _____ 6 wait _____

2 talk _____ 7 shout _____

3 walk _____ 8 play _____

4 paint _____ 9 close _____

5 sprinkle _____ 10 open _____

C Rewrite each of these short phrases in the past tense.

1 sail the yacht _____

2 lift the case _____

3 enjoy the sunshine _____

4 turn the key _____

5 follow the map _____

6 laugh at the clown _____

7 scratch the car _____

8 gasp for air _____

9 walk home _____

10 wait for me _____

Skills Unit 4

Skills Book Aims:

1 To suggest alternative words to *got*.

2 To introduce collective nouns.

3 To teach the appropriate use of *I* and *me*.

4 To practise the *ear* spelling pattern.

5 To practise making codes.

Tudor and Stuart pastimes

Teaching notes

Stimulus	Joseph Nash print; historical description; pictures	Discuss and compare sports and pastimes of the Tudor and Stuart period with those of today. Encourage debate about such issues as animal cruelty in 'sport'.
Comprehension	cloze; literal; inferential	See general note in introduction, page 5.
Vocabulary	over-used words (*got*)	*Got*, together with *nice* and *lot*, is perpetually over-used by children at this stage in their writing. **Pcm 1** gives an opportunity for further practice in looking for a more interesting word.
Punctuation/ Grammar	collective nouns; subject and predicate	**Pcm 2**, in which the children are seeking collective nouns to use in place of 'a lot of', follows naturally from **pcm 1**. Encourage the use of dictionaries in this activity. Some teachers may be inclined to shy away from the terms 'subject' and 'predicate', but the concepts as required in **NE** are quite simple, as can be seen in the description in the pupils' text (page 18). An understanding of the *subject* (usually the person or thing doing the action of the verb) and the *predicate* (the rest of the sentence) clarifies when to use *I* and when to use *me* in a sentence. **Pcm 3** supports these teaching points. Note that at this stage the complications of passive sentences have not been taken into account.
Spelling	*ear* pattern	The activities build on work at earlier levels which focused on *ea* pattern words. A group might paint a large picture of a face for a wall display. On each of two very large ears words can be written corresponding to the two phonemes associated here with the pattern, which are practised in the pupils' exercises.
Quiz	decoding messages	Children are invited to make their own codes. Encourage them to make letter-to-letter codes, as well as letter-to-number codes.

Answers

Comprehension

A 1 Yachting, horse racing and hunting are options.
  2 village green
  3 football
  4 fishing

B 1 Two sports which are against the law today are bear-baiting and cock-fighting.
  2 Maypole dancing, bowls and fairs took place on the village green.
  3 Most people went to bed early and got up early in the morning because they only had candles and oil lamps to light their rooms at night so they made the best possible use of daylight.
  4 (Individual answers.)

Vocabulary – over-used words: *got*

A In 1665 a terrible illness called the plague **affected** many people. If you **contracted** it you **became** very sick. Parents **felt** worried if their children **caught** it as they might die. All ill people had to stay indoors. The law said you must burn the bed of the sick person. They had no other ways to stop the disease.

Grammar – collective nouns

A 1 choir
  2 throng/multitude/mob/ crowd
  3 bunch
  4 forest/copse
  5 flock
  6 fleet/flotilla/convoy
  7 litter
  8 troop/platoon/company/ army

B 1 playing musical instruments
  2 waiting
  3 watching a performance
  4 performing in a theatrical/ dance production
  5 praying/worshipping
  6 being noisy/rowdy/ disorderly
  7 manual work/working on a ship or aeroplane
  8 singing/dancing

C 1 sheep/birds
  2 bees/wasps
  3 sticks (firewood)/rags
  4 stars
  5 lions
  6 geese
  7 cows/animals
  8 animals

Grammar – subject and predicate using 'I' and 'me'

A 1 I have a sister called Ruth.
  2 Our friends are waiting for Ben and me.
  3 Jamie, Lisa and I are going to town today.
  4 Can Asif and I come with you?
  5 Do you want to come with Mum and me?

Spelling – *ear* pattern

A **learnt**   **fear**
   search   ear
   earn   hear
   earth   clear
   early   near
   earl   rear
   pearl
   learn

Quiz – decoding messages

1 SEND A CODED MESSAGE TO A FRIEND
2 E (opinion)

See also: **p.85**, **Development** notes.

Nelson English — SKILLS BOOK 3 — Unit 4 — Pcm 1

name _____ date _____

A better word?

Write these again, using a better word than *got*, *nice* or *lot*.

1. a nice cake _____
2. She got a new shirt. _____
3. a nice tune _____
4. He got ill. _____
5. a nice meal _____
6. that lot of birds _____
7. a nice garden _____
8. She got a bus. _____
9. a nice face _____
10. a lot of bees _____

Nelson English — SKILLS BOOK 3 — Unit 4 — Pcm 2

name _____ date _____

Collective nouns

Choose the *collective noun* that you could use in place of *lot* in these phrases.

1. a lot of cows _____ party / herd / clump
2. a lot of ships _____ swarm / convoy / flight
3. a lot of flowers _____ bunch / packet / cluster
4. a lot of people _____ crowd / herd / swarm
5. a lot of sailors _____ army / crew / gaggle
6. a lot of sheep _____ school / team / flock
7. a lot of musicians _____ team / band / crowd
8. a lot of furniture _____ pile / suite / bundle

Published by Thomas Nelson and Sons Ltd 1995

Nelson English © John Jackman and Wendy Wren 1995.

Subjects and predicates

The *subject* of the sentence tells us who or what it is about. The *predicate* tells us what the subject does, or what happens to the subject.

A Underline the subjects in these sentences. The first is done for you.

1 <u>The water</u> is too shallow for diving.

2 The player threw the ball.

3 The referee said it was a penalty.

4 The team looked smart before the match started.

B Add a subject to each predicate to make a sentence.

1 _____ play netball.

2 _____ can run very quickly.

3 _____ passed the ball.

4 _____ won the game.

C Fill in the gaps using *I* or *me*.

1 _____ am a good runner.

2 Ali is a better swimmer than _____ .

3 James and _____ are going to watch the match.

4 Joe came to watch _____ play.

5 Mum bought new boots for Ben and _____ .

Skills Unit 5

Skills Book Aims:

1. To use word shape to help to convey meaning.
2. To extend knowledge of antonyms.
3. To practise using the main punctuation marks.
4. To introduce the concept of conjunctions.
5. To practise the *soft c* spelling patterns.

Wings

Teaching notes

Stimulus	factual text; photographs; pictures	Information books on birds are among the most popular in children's libraries. This unit has been devised to look in detail at one aspect of this topic. Encourage the collection of information and reference books, and other sources to which the class may have access.
Comprehension	cloze; literal; inferential	See general note in introduction, page 5.
Vocabulary	word shapes; antonyms	Making word shapes, in whatever medium is appropriate, can be a rewarding art or craft activity. Extension of the work on antonyms is available on **pcm 1**.
Punctuation/ Grammar	punctuation marks; conjunctions; compound sentences	This short activity practises all the main punctuation forms previously introduced, including direct speech. The grammar activity extends the earlier work on conjunctions, and begins to develop the concept of compound sentences. **Pcm 2** first practises the use of simple conjunctions, and part **B** focuses on making interesting compound sentences from several short 'simple' sentences about the same subject. Extend the work further by suggesting the children look back at recent pieces of writing to see whether, in the light of this work on conjunctions and compound sentences, there are any groups of short sentences that they might now choose to edit.
Spelling	soft *c*	Make a class anthology of limericks written for this spelling group. Groups of children could be assigned other spelling patterns for limerick writing.
Quiz	word puzzle	Challenge the children to produce their own puzzles for each other on the same basis.

Answers

Comprehension

A 1 long
  2 short
  3 wide
  4 soaring

B 1 The wings of a gull are long and slim.
  2 The albatross can sleep while it flies.
  3 Birds of prey need to soar high in the sky so they can look for food.
  4 (The plane in the photograph is a glider so the children will say that it glides.)

Vocabulary – word shapes

A (Individually drawn answers.)

Vocabulary – antonyms

A high – low
  in – out
  short – tall/long
  straight – crooked/bent/curved
  up – down
  top – bottom
  wide – narrow
  below – above
  cover – uncover
  fair – unfair
  lucky – unlucky
  honest – dishonest
  correct – incorrect
  efficient – inefficient

Punctuation – punctuation marks

A 1 Sparrows, starlings, kingfishers and woodpeckers all have short wings.
  2 Do you enjoy bird-watching?
  3 The huge albatross has long, sleek, graceful wings.
  4 "This bird has a broken wing," said the old lady.
  5 "In Jamaica," said Wesley dreamily, "the birds have such wonderful colours."

Grammar – conjunctions / compound sentences

A 1 Humans can fly **but** they need machines to help them.
  2 The bird flies fast **and** it catches the moth.
  3 The kestrel hovers over a mouse **but** the little animal escapes.
  4 Kestrels can hover or fly quickly **but** Concorde can only fly quickly.
  5 I like bird-watching **and** I enjoy drawing birds.

B 1 I hid behind the hedge **so/until** I could see the birds.
  2 The keeper wears a thick glove **because** the eagle has sharp claws.
  3 The gull glided along the cliff **until** it reached its nesting place.
  4 Short wings are good for twisting and turning **but** long wings are better for gliding.

Spelling – soft *c*

A (Individual answers.)

Quiz – puzzle it out

1 seat, eats
2 speak, peaks
3 horse, shore
4 stun, nuts

See also: **p.87**, Development notes.

Nelson SKILLS BOOK 3
Unit 5
ENGLISH Pcm 1   name _____ date _____

Antonyms

A Circle the word at the end of each sentence which is the *antonym* of the word underlined.

1 We all had a good laugh.   smile / cry

2 They had wanted clean shirts for the match.   dirty / fresh

3 They thought looking good would help them win.   play / lose

4 Bob's Dad said starch would brighten the colours.   darken / change

5 He was mistaken.   wrong / right

6 Now they couldn't stop laughing.   end / start

7 The team had the only stiff shirts in the league.   solid / limp

B Sort the words in the box into pairs which are antonyms.

remember	fail	lose	retreat	stop	slow	catch
find	discourage	tie	prohibit	damage	succeed
advance	allow	start	shout	fast	drop	forget
encourage	untie	repair	whisper

_____ _____ _____ _____
_____ _____ _____ _____
_____ _____ _____ _____
_____ _____ _____ _____
_____ _____ _____ _____
_____ _____ _____ _____

C Find an antonym for the underlined word in each phrase.

1 hard question _____
2 buy a computer _____
3 correct answer _____
4 cool breeze _____
5 east wind _____
6 calm sea _____
7 rough fur _____
8 noisy music _____

Published by Thomas Nelson and Sons Ltd 1995   Nelson English © John Jackman and Wendy Wren 1995.

Conjunctions

A Combine these pairs of sentences. The first is done to help you.

1 We have to go to school. We mustn't be late.

We have to go to school and we mustn't be late.

2 Our class is organising the assembly. I am reading a poem.

3 I wanted to read a story. My teacher said I had to read a poem.

B Combine these sentences into one sentence.

1 Kate read a story. It was long. It was boring.

2 Greg held up his picture. It was a colourful picture. It showed birds flying.

3 I didn't like my poem. My poem was about flying. All the other children thought it was good poem.

C Write three short sentences about a bird. Then combine them into one sentence.

Skills Unit 6

The Ganges - a holy river

Skills Book Aims:

1. To develop adjectives derived from country names.
2. To revise the punctuation of direct speech.
3. To introduce the *i* before *e* spelling rule.

Teaching notes

Stimulus	factual text; photographs; pictures	This topic would be enhanced by inviting parents or other visitors with first-hand experience of the Ganges, to talk to the class. Several interesting aspects of the unit may be explored in greater depth, such as the life-styles of the holy men.
Comprehension	cloze; literal; inferential	See general note in introduction, page 5.
Vocabulary	adjectives made from countries	After this section of the unit has been completed, try a 'quick quiz' dictation, mixing the different types of adjectival endings which have been taught.
Punctuation/ Grammar	direct speech	Although this has been the subject of several activities in earlier units and books, direct speech requires considerable reinforcement. Thus, not only is it returned to in the text, but there are two **pcms** to support the understanding of this skill for those children requiring additional help.
Spelling	*i* before *e*	This is the first introduction to this well-known 'rule', which is returned to as one of the **NE** *"12 Tips for Better Spelling"* in **Skills Book 5**. Here, as there, the children should realise that whilst such spelling rules, if properly applied, will ensure their spellings are more often right than wrong, the rules are not absolute. They should therefore learn each rule, but also try to memorise the exceptions!
Quiz	world rivers	Mark the rivers on a large outline map of the world. Have fun teaching the children how to remember the spelling of *Mississippi*.

Answers

Comprehension

A 1 Ganges
 2 Hindu
 3 six
 4 Calcutta

B 1 Two hundred million people live in the Ganges Valley.
 2 People want to journey along the Ganges because they believe it is a holy river.
 3 Varanasi is famous as a holy city which has many beautiful temples and religious museums.
 4 (Opinion: risk of flood damage, over-population so pressure on land use.)

Vocabulary – adjectives made from countries

A 1 Jamaican
 2 Australian
 3 Canadian
 4 American
 5 Ugandan
 6 Russian

B 1 Spanish
 2 Scottish
 3 Chinese
 4 Swedish

C 1 Germany
 2 Wales
 3 Belgium
 4 Greece
 5 Pakistan
 6 France
 7 Norway
 8 Burma

Punctuation – direct speech

A 1 "You must not enter the temple with shoes on," said Rajiv.
 2 Father said, "These waters have special powers."
 3 "My parents live in Delhi," said Reena.
 4 "Would you like to visit Varanasi?" asked the guide.
 5 "Be careful," shouted the fisherman, "or you'll damage my nets!"

Spelling – *i* before *e*

Across: pier, weir/weird, receive, thief, relief/lie, yield

Down: pier, heir, chief, receipt, field, vie/view, deceive, sieve, height

Quiz – world rivers

(Atlas work.)

See also: **p.89**, Development notes.

SKILLS BOOK 3
Unit 6
Pcm 1

name _____   date _____

Using direct speech (1)

Look at these pictures. Write what each speaker said. Use the words **said** or **asked** and the name of the speaker in your answers. Don't forget to use inverted commas, commas and full stops where they are needed. The first is done to help you.

1. What are you doing on Saturday?

2. Dad is taking my sister and me to watch football.

3. I am going to visit my Gran in London.

4. I'm going to Matt's party.

1 What did the teacher say?

"What are you doing on Saturday?" asked the teacher.

2 What did Mark say?

_____

3 What did Khalid say?

_____

4 What did Vicky say?

_____

Using direct speech (2)

A Add the inverted commas which are missing from these sentences.

I have lost my dog, said Phil.

Put an advert in the paper, said Delroy.

Don't be silly, he can't read, said Phil.

Why does an ostrich have a long neck? asked Zoe.

I don't know, said Gurmit.

Because its head is so far from its body, laughed Zoe.

Why do sheep have woolly coats? asked Winston.

They would look silly in plastic macs, said the farmer.

B Add the inverted commas, commas, full stops and question marks that are missing from these sentences.

Why did you throw that clock out of the window asked Carl

I wanted to see time fly replied Sue

Pete asked What's your new dog's name

Grandad replied Don't know, he won't tell me

Our baby is only a year old said Susie and he has been walking since he was nine months

Really replied Annie he must be very tired by now

Skills Unit 7

Skills Book Aims:

1 To introduce similes.

2 To practise the structure of a personal letter.

3 To practise irregular past tense verb forms.

4 To practise the *ure* spelling pattern.

How Mowgli joined the wolves

Teaching notes

Stimulus	narrative text – classic children's fiction; pictures	Read further extracts to the class, or encourage some children to read the rest of *Mowgli's Brothers* and/or other stories for themselves.
Comprehension	cloze; literal; inferential	See general note in introduction, page 5.
Vocabulary	similes	Collect as many similes as possible. Organise a competition to find who can produce the funniest picture which illustrates a simile taken literally!
Punctuation/ Grammar	letter writing; verbs/past tense	This is the first occasion on which all the structural aspects of letter writing are brought together. Extend and practise by writing 'real' letters to a family friend or relative. This may need a certain amount of advance preparation to ensure the availability of relevant addresses. Make two lists of verbs in their present and past tenses – one for those which take the regular form (+*d* or +*ed*), and one for those whose middle vowel is changed. **Pcms** 1 and 2 support these suggestions and activities.
Spelling	*ure* pattern	Look up each of the listed *ure* words in a dictionary to check the full definitions against those offered in the unit activity.
Quiz	animal match – adjectives	Take one or two of the words and see how many other relevant adjectives can be collected. A useful activity for paired or group work.

Answers

Comprehension

A 1 four
2 laughed
3 never
4 egg

B 1 The baby pushed his way between the cubs "to get close to the warm hide" (to reach Mother Wolf and get food and warmth, just like her cubs).
2 (Opinion: The writer describes the child as 'a little atom' because the child is small, very young and could easily be hurt in this situation.)
3 Mowgli was named after Mowgli the Frog.
4 (Opinion: Mother Wolf was very keen to keep Mowgli because she was impressed and touched by his courage and trust.)

Vocabulary – similes

A 1 rock
2 arrow
3 snow
4 grass
5 tortoise

B (Individual answers.)

Punctuation – letter writing

A (Individual letters.)

Grammar – verbs in the past tense

A swam, said, ran, stole, bit, sang, gave, found, fell, threw

B was   stood
woke   came
scratched looked
yawned   laughed
spread   closed
lay   scratched
said   laid
rustled   was pushing
dropped   gasped
snapped

C The wolf jumped up as he heard the rustle. He wondered what it was (might be). He was amazed when he saw it was a tiny baby. It was standing (stood) nearby, holding (and held) a low branch.

Spelling – *ure* pattern

B 1 puncture
2 vulture
3 adventure
4 secure
5 pasture
6 furniture
7 creature
8 fracture
9 picture
10 signature

Quiz – animal match

(Individual answers, but suggestions are:)
1 fierce, stripy, hungry, rare
2 slow, shy, sleepy
3 big, huge, heavy
4 tiny, quiet, quick
5 hungry, ugly, scrawny
6 small, tiny, loud, noisy
7 rare, beautiful, fierce
8 placid, patient, nervous

See also: **p.91**, Development notes. 43

Nelson ENGLISH SKILLS BOOK 3 **Unit 7** Pcm 1

name _____ date _____

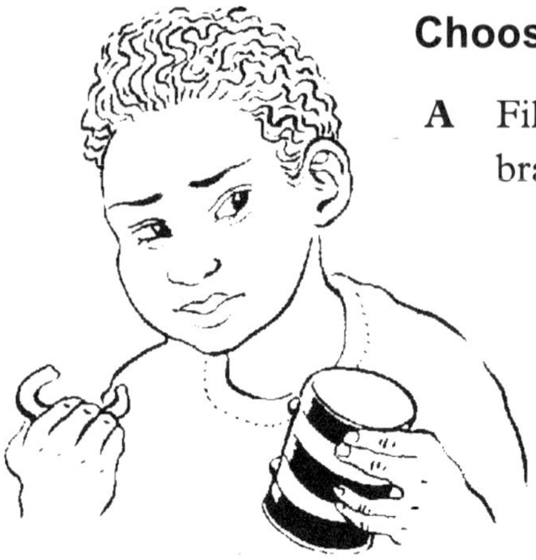

Choosing the right word

A Fill the gap in each sentence with the correct word in the brackets.

1 My baby brother _____ well to learn the rhyme.   (done/did)

2 Mum and Dad _____ very pleased with him.   (was/were)

3 They had not _____ that he had broken his new mug.   (saw/seen)

4 Now they _____ not pleased with him.   (are/is)

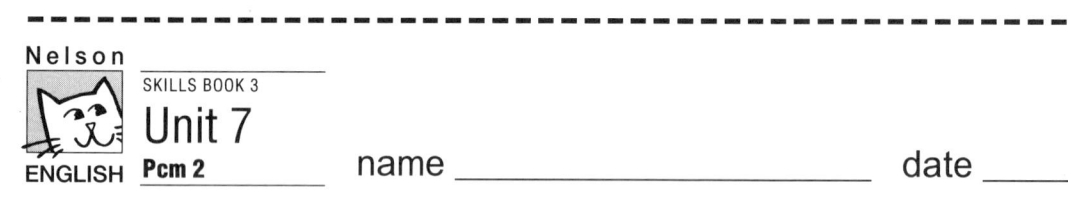

Nelson ENGLISH SKILLS BOOK 3 **Unit 7** Pcm 2

name _____ date _____

Past tense

Fill in the gaps in these sentences. Each sentence is about something which has happened in the past. The verbs in brackets will help you.

1 Dad (come) _____ to watch me play.

2 The game (begin) _____ well.

3 I (kick) _____ the ball at the goal.

4 It (go) _____ over the bar.

5 My teacher (say) _____ ,"Bad luck!"

6 I (know) _____ we could win.

7 I suddenly (see) _____ my chance.

8 I (run) _____ as fast as I could.

9 The ball (land) _____ right at my feet.

10 I (score) _____ the winner, and Dad saw me!

Published by Thomas Nelson and Sons Ltd 1995

Nelson English © John Jackman and Wendy Wren 1995.

Skills Unit 8

Skills Book Aims:

1. To practise classifications.
2. To revise and extend synonyms.
3. To revise the main elements of sentence punctuation.
4. To teach plural forms of words ending with *o*.

Fire beneath our feet

Teaching notes

Stimulus	factual text; photograph; diagram; picture	Due to their dramatic and potentially devastating characteristics, volcanoes fascinate many children. They also lend themselves to some impressive photography, being one of the few earth forms which can be created, and sometimes destroyed, in a very short space of time. The processes involved are essentially simple, easily understood, and so form a useful introduction to the evolution of our landscape which, as with our language, is in a constant state of change.
Comprehension	cloze; literal; inferential	See general note in introduction, page 5.
Vocabulary	synonyms	This activity, which is supported by **pcm 1**, lays the foundation for thesaurus work in future units in this book. Thus any reinforcement of the concept, such as by playing short fill-in oral quiz games with the class, will be of value.
Punctuation/ Grammar	sentences; direct speech	Using the direct speech activity, together with the stimulus material, in pairs or groups the children could create short drama sequences, imagining that during a visit to an apparently extinct volcano, they get caught up in what seems to be the early stages of an eruption. Afterwards they could transcribe this in simple drama script form, or write it as a short story with heavy emphasis on direct speech.
Spelling	plurals/words ending in *o*	**Pcm 2** gives the opportunity for further practice. The riddle answer is "potatoes", in the context of this section, but children who answer "needles" are correct too.
Quiz	punctuation puzzle	All the punctuation and word spaces have been omitted. Similar puzzles can be easily constructed, by either the teacher or the children, primarily as another device to ensure ample revision of the main punctuation and capitalisation rules.

Answers

Comprehension

A 1 hot
  2 magma
  3 Volcanoes
  4 Arthur's Seat

B 1 The rocks in the centre of the Earth are 'like thick syrup' because they are extremely hot and have melted.
  2 'Magma' is known as 'lava' when it escapes onto the surface of the Earth.
  3 A 'simile' in the passage is "like thick syrup"/"like a cork in a bottle".
  4 An extinct volcano is one that is no longer active, that is so old that the magma deep in the Earth has stopped trying to reach the surface.

Vocabulary – odd-one-out

A 1 Sugar; the others are types of mineral and this is made (by and) from plants.
  2 Church; the others are natural features and this is man-made.
  3 Grass; the others are to do with volcanoes and this is a plant.
  4 Wood; the others are liquid and this is solid.

Vocabulary – synonyms

A 1 melted
  2 middle
  3 dead
  4 very

Punctuation – sentences

A 1 There are volcanoes in Iceland.
  2 Have you ever been to Edinburgh?
  3 Ouch, that was hot!
  4 The hot, swirling, molten lava engulfed the houses.

Punctuation – direct speech

A 2 "You may find it a steep climb up," he said. "However, it's an easy walk down."
  3 "If you look carefully," he shouted, "you will be able to see the lava bubbling."
  4 Tom was scared. "I don't like being so close to a volcano," he said.

Spelling – plurals/words ending in *o*

A heroes, cockatoos, bamboo (bamboos is correct but rarely used), echoes, altos, tomatoes, mottoes, sopranos, photos, cellos, potatoes

Quiz

There are no active volcanoes in Britain but there are some extinct ones like Arthur's Seat in Edinburgh.

See also: **p.93, Development** notes.

Synonyms

A Colour the box containing the word which is a *synonym* of the first word in each row. Use a dictionary to help you. The first is done to help you.

observe	watch	find	listen	throw
enemy	friend	foe	gang	men
smell	bad	sweet	odour	scent
weary	energetic	tired	hungry	dirty
terror	ghost	bad	dark	fear
change	alter	give	find	clothes

B Rewrite these sentences, finding a synonym for each of the words underlined.

1 "The bus times had been altered," I pleaded.

2 "That is a feeble excuse for being late," said my teacher.

3 "You won't be selected for the team if you're late again," he said.

4 I thought he was being very unjust.

5 I made certain to be at school on time from then on!

Nelson English SKILLS BOOK 3 Unit 8 Pcm 2

name _____ date _____

Words ending with o

Write the plural of each of these words.

1 patio _____   4 radio _____   7 cello _____

2 solo _____   5 piano _____   8 potato _____

3 echo _____   6 hero _____   9 banjo _____

Fill the gaps in these sentences using the words from the exercise which you have just done.

1 Dad was peeling the _____ for lunch.

2 He was listening to one of his portable _____ .

3 His greatest _____ are musicians.

4 He loves to listen to the twang of _____ .

5 He makes us listen to _____ and guess which instruments are playing.

6 _____ look like big violins, but are difficult to pick out.

7 _____ are much easier as they are usually played alone.

RIDDLE?

Riddle: What have eyes but cannot see?

_____

Published by Thomas Nelson and Sons Ltd 1995   Nelson English © John Jackman and Wendy Wren 1995.

Skills Unit 9

Skills Book Aims:

1. To introduce prefix *al*.
2. To introduce suffix *ful*.
3. To consider paragraphs as relating to one main idea.
4. To introduce plural possessive nouns.
5. To teach the *are* spelling pattern.
6. To illustrate and use sign language.

Fire!

Teaching notes

Stimulus	photographs; factual text; pictures	The photographs and text about Falklands veteran Simon Weston are intended to help the children begin to explore some of the implications of disablement. Encourage the children to discuss and share their experiences/anxieties about being disabled and, if feasible, invite a disabled person or someone from an organisation concerned with the disabled (e.g. Phab, RNIB) to share or discuss the social, physical and emotional experiences or implications.
Comprehension	cloze; literal; inferential	See general note in introduction, page 5.
Vocabulary	word origins; suffix (*ful*)	This pairing focuses on the common difficulty associated with both patterns, namely the dropping of the second *l* from what might be expected. **Pcm 1** offers examples, and demonstrates how other prefixes and suffixes change word meaning.
Punctuation/ Grammar	paragraphs; possessive nouns	As is noted elsewhere, there are different schools of thought as to the appropriate setting out of paragraphs. The style adopted in **Nelson English** is to indent the first line of each paragraph. However, the children may notice the convention that the first paragraph in printed material (as in the stimulus material) is not usually indented. Similarly, it can be pointed out that with the growth of word processing, the conventions are changing to favour first lines being 'full out', with a line space between paragraphs. This offers an opportunity to discuss the critical factor, namely that what really matters is clarity in communication of meaning to the reader, this being the important question when seeking to determine which of the two methods is better. **Pcm 2** extends the work on possessive nouns.
Spelling	*are* pattern	Extend by writing a paragraph or poem, such as a limerick, about a fireworks party. Include as many *are* words as possible.
Quiz	sign language	Pairs might enjoy communicating with each other using the finger signs. Notice the pattern of the vowel letters.

Answers

Comprehension

A 1 clothes
2 face
3 hide
4 medal

B 1 (Individual answer.)
2 He wanted to talk to lots of people to tell them how he felt, and because he wanted to encourage people to treat disabled and disfigured people normally and to help them.
3 (Individual answer.)
4 (Opinion: I think that Simon's family are proud of him because of his bravery and eagerness to help others.)

Vocabulary – suffix *ful*

A 1 painful
2 useful
3 hopeful
4 wonderful

Grammar – paragraphs

A (Individual answers, focussing on the fire at a family home, the trapped child, the anxious mother and child waiting below the window, the fire brigade working to put out the fire, and a firefighter rescuing the trapped child and carrying him/her down the ladder.)

Grammar – possessive nouns

A 1 the firefighter's helmet
2 the fire engine's siren
3 Simon's face
4 the blind person's dog

B 1 my three friends' houses
2 the parents' meeting
3 the four birds' nests
4 my two cousins' bikes

C 1 the children's home
2 the herd's leader
3 the men's club
4 the disabled people's coach
5 our twins' birthday
6 the firefighters' helmets

Spelling – *are* pattern

A beware, scared, careful, flare

B *Across*
1 spare
3 rare

Down
1 square
2 fare

Quiz – sign language

1 HELLO
2 THANKS
3 BYE

See also: **p.95**, **Development** notes.

Prefixes and suffixes

re means *again* so **re**do means *do again*

pre- means *before* **mis-** means *wrongly* or *not*

-able means *that can be* **-less** means *without*

-ness means *being*

A Write your definition for these words.

1 kind**ness** _____

2 **re**make _____

3 **mis**understand _____

4 help**less** _____

5 lov**able** _____

6 **pre**date _____

B Adding the prefixes **dis** and **un** can make the word have the opposite meaning (antonym).

Make the antonyms of these words, using **dis** or **un**.

1 likely _____ 2 obey _____

3 wrap _____ 4 fair _____

5 approve _____ 6 tidy _____

7 happy _____ 8 respect _____

9 mount _____ 10 even _____

11 honest _____ 12 known _____

Possessive nouns

Fill in this chart. The first row has been done to help you.

Noun	Plural	Singular possessive	Plural possessive
cat	cats	cat's	cats'
boy			
dog			
teacher			
doctor			
child			
man			
woman			

Rewrite these sentences, but use a possessive noun in place of the words underlined.

1 The cat of our teacher has two kittens.

2 The colours of the kittens are black and white.

3 The parents of David said he could have one.

4 The mother of my friends said they could have one too.

5 The parents of the other children would not let them.

Skills Unit 10

Skills Book Aims:

1 To help distinguish between *where*, *were* and *we're*.

2 To introduce verbs whose past tense is irregular.

3 To practise the *able* spelling pattern.

Victorian homes

Teaching notes

Stimulus	factual text; photographs; illustrations	This important history topic lends itself to drama and oral discussion work which can encourage empathy with children who lived in Victorian times. Encourage the children to consider both the benefits as well as the more readily identifiable disadvantages of life in the 19th century. Make collections of Victoriana, which can be used for descriptive and imaginative writing.
Comprehension	cloze; literal; inferential	See general note in introduction, page 5.
Vocabulary	*where, were, we're*	Whilst these three words frequently lead to confusion, they are not homophones. However the work can be developed to look at other words of a similar character which may cause confusion, most of which are homophones. **Pcm 1** gives some examples.
Punctuation/ Grammar	past tense	Collect a class verb bank, like a bottle bank. Cut out bottle shapes from two different colours of paper. On one colour write verbs in their present and past tense which are regular (i.e. they simply require the addition of *d* or *ed* to form the past tense) and on the other write verbs which are irregular.
Spelling	*able* pattern	Some children will enjoy trying to establish a pattern to determine the conditions which lead to the final *e* not being dropped before adding the suffix *able*, which is the norm. It occurs when the word ends in a vowel digraph such as *ee* (e.g. agreeable) or where the word ends in *ce* or *ge* (e.g. peaceable). See also Unit 10a, **pcm 2**.
Quiz	jumbled words – word order	Similar quizzes may be constructed by the children for each other to unravel.

Answers

Comprehension

A 1 poor
 2 rivers
 3 soap
 4 gardens; toilets

B 1 There was so much disease amongst the poor because they often lived in small, damp houses in filthy, rat-infested narrow streets and alleys, and they shared outdoor 'earth closets' for toilets so sewage often seeped into their water supplies.

 2 Robert Owen and the Lever brothers built better houses for their workers because they realised that their workers would work better if they were healthy, had comfortable homes and were well-fed.
 3 People moved to live in the towns to try to get work in the new factories there.
 4 (Individual answer.)

Vocabulary – *where, were* and *we're*

A 1 were, were
 2 We're, where
 3 where
 4 were
 5 were, where

B (Individual answers.)

Grammar – past tense

A come/came
 steal/stole
 find/found
 fall/fell
 swim/swam
 wear/wore
 have/had
 eat/ate
 sink/sank

B 2 Most children ate sweets.
 3 Some men wore hats.
 4 The snow settled thickly on the ground.
 5 People had to work hard to earn money.
 6 Children swam in the river.
 7 She sold flowers.
 8 Some people found it difficult to buy enough food.

Spelling – *able* pattern

A 1 (Individual answer.)
 2 (Individual answers.)
 3 (Individual work.)

Quiz – jumbled words

Victorian, houses, factories, workers, money, families

See also: **p.96**, **Development** notes.

Same sound, different meaning

A These pairs of sentences contain pairs of *homophones*. One is given to you. Write the other in the gap. Check your answers by using a dictionary.

1 I fell in the <u>hole</u>. The _____ class is in the play.

2 I <u>knew</u> his brother. He broke my _____ game.

3 She always thinks she is <u>right</u>. Turn _____ by the shops.

4 Mum's taking us to the <u>fair</u>. The bus _____ is 80p.

5 I bought it cheap in the <u>sale</u>. The yacht has a red _____ .

6 Gran does not <u>hear</u> well. Come and sit _____ .

7 My dog has a short <u>tail</u>. I enjoy a good fairy _____ .

8 <u>There</u> will be trouble. We visited _____ house.

9 This is a dense <u>wood</u>. He said he _____ help me.

10 He <u>threw</u> the stick. I walked _____ the door.

B Look at these pairs of homophones. The definition of the first one is given; write the definition of the second. Use a dictionary to help you.

1 *hair* the growth that covers the head

   hare _____

2 *beech* a large tree

   beach _____

3 *meet* to come together

   meat _____

4 *stairs* a set of steps

   stares _____

5 *weight* heaviness

   wait _____

Skills Unit 10a

Skills Book Aims:

1 To introduce the concept of root words.

2 To extend the understanding of conjunctions.

3 To teach the correct use of *who* and *which*.

4 To practise the *ible* spelling pattern.

5 To introduce palindromes.

Victorian fashion

Teaching notes

Stimulus	factual text; captioned pictures; picture sequence	Discuss the various functions of clothes in Victorian times, including warmth, protection and social differentiation. Debate whether similar functional distinctions exist in our times, such as fashions adopted by different age groups. Some children may be able to bring to school very early family photos. Consider the impracticality of the crinoline, and other more recent inconvenient fashions.
Comprehension	cloze; literal; inferential	See general note in introduction, page 5.
Vocabulary	root words	Fun can be had illustrating the 'silly' sentences, as is exemplified by the artwork on page 50.
Punctuation/ Grammar	conjunctions; *who* and *which*	Using conjunctions to connect short, simple sentences is one of the more immediately effective ways for children to improve the general flow of their writing. Invite them to look over a piece of their own earlier writing where this device might have been profitably employed, and to rewrite part or all of the piece concerned. However, warn them about the trap of over-extending their sentences! **Pcm 1** gives opportunities to practise the use of *who* and *which*.
Spelling	*ible* pattern	**Pcm 2** practises both the *ible* and the *able* pattern.
Quiz	palindromes	This is introduced as another example of playing with language, both to increase familiarity, and also to have fun for its own sake.

Answers

Comprehension

A 1 warm
  2 hat
  3 caps
  4 crinolines

B 1 Bankers and factory owners usually wore top hats.
  2 The invention of new colour dyes particularly affected women's fashion during the Victorian period.
  3 The 1890s were called the mauve decade because mauve dyes were so popular then.
  4 (Opinion: I think the crinoline soon became unpopular because it was so big and awkward to wear.)

Vocabulary – root words

A 1 (Individual answers.)
  2 (Individual answer.)

Grammar – using conjunctions

A 1 and, but, yet, although, though, when, while
  2 but, although, when, as, yet, though, after
  3 because, for, as, when, while
  4 or
  5 and, but, although, though, after, yet, when

Grammar – using *who* and *which*

A 1 This is my Uncle Bill who works in the mine.
  2 He wanted a new hat which would keep him warm.
  3 We met a farmer who had two sheepdogs.
  4 I have two rabbits which I feed every day.

Spelling – *ible* endings

A (Individual answers.)

Quiz – palindromes

1 WAS IT A CAT I SAW?
  A MAN, A PLAN, A CANAL, PANAMA.
2 (Individual work.)

See also: **p.96**, **Development** notes.

SKILLS BOOK 3
Unit 10a
Pcm 1

name _____ date _____

Using *who* and *which*

A Fill in the gaps in these sentences with either **who** or **which**.

On the way to school we saw a policeman _____ was directing the traffic. We walked past the park _____ has swings and a slide. We saw Jenny _____ was wearing her new trousers. She was walking her new puppy _____ she had collected only yesterday. The wind was blowing hard _____ made the little animal excitable. It ran into the road, _____ was busy with traffic. Jenny, _____ was holding the lead tightly, quickly pulled the puppy back.

B Use **who** or **which** to join each of these pairs of sentences.

1 At school I saw Emma and Steven. They are my cousins.

2 They were wearing new gloves. Their Mum had knitted them.

3 They are in Miss Walsh's class. It is for younger children.

4 My best friend is Ashok. He sits next to me.

5 We help each other with maths. It is difficult.

Published by Thomas Nelson and Sons Ltd 1995   Nelson English © John Jackman and Wendy Wren 1995.

Nelson English — SKILLS BOOK 3 — Unit 10a — Pcm 2

name _____ date _____

able and ible

A Choose the word from the box which finishes these sentences.

| breakable | washable | reversible |
| incredible | possible | readable |

1 Something that can be broken if dropped is _____.

2 A coat that can be worn with either side out is _____.

3 Something that can be easily read is _____.

4 Something which is unbelievable is _____.

5 An activity that can be done is _____.

6 Clothes which can be cleaned in water are _____.

B Underline each word with a suffix **able** or **ible**. Then write its root word on the line.

1 I find swimming very enjoyable. _____

2 It is important to be sensible in the pool. _____

3 Mum makes me responsible for my brother. _____

4 Luckily he is very reliable. _____

5 The indoor pool is usable all year round. _____

6 Mum is agreeable to our buying crisps. _____

Published by Thomas Nelson and Sons Ltd 1995   Nelson English © John Jackman and Wendy Wren 1995.

Skills Unit 11

Skills Book Aims:

1. To introduce comparative forms of longer adjectives.
2. To practise setting out conversations within text.
3. To practise the *tion* pattern.
4. To identify rhyme from sound rather than letter patterns.

Travelling the River Amazon

Teaching notes

Stimulus	short narrative; photographs; pictures	The Amazon is not only the biggest river on Earth, it is also one of the most fascinating. There are many aspects which the children can research, leading to a variety of creative and expressive activities. This is also a particularly appropriate subject around which library and note-taking skills can be taught and practised.
Comprehension	cloze; literal; inferential	See general note in introduction, page 5.
Vocabulary	comparatives	**Pcm 1** provides opportunities to support the work on comparative forms, including the use of *more*.
Punctuation/ Grammar	conversations	Writing conversations can require considerable reinforcement. Thus it can be helpful to use passages similar to that provided in this unit, either as teacher-produced **pcms**, or simply written on the board, as a task for the children to complete at a convenient time during the day between other activities.
Spelling	*tion* pattern	**Pcm 2** gives practice in a range of contexts. If a word ends in *t*, explain that this should not be doubled when adding the suffix.
Quiz	rhyme	Look through poetry books to find words which rhyme but which also have different spelling patterns.

Answers

Comprehension

A 1 Amazon
   2 strong
   3 bananas
   4 anaconda

B 1 Paco knows a storm is coming because the wind makes waves in the River Amazon.
   2 When the birds and animals sense danger they are silent.
   3 (Opinion: I would feel nervous/scared about swimming in the River Amazon because of the piranhas, anacondas and electric eels.)
   4 (Opinion.)

Vocabulary – comparatives

A 1 busy = busier
   2 heavy = heavier
   3 dirty = dirtier
   4 mighty = mightier
   5 noisy = noisier
   6 pretty = prettier
   7 dusty = dustier
   8 lively = livelier

Vocabulary – adding *more*

A 2 more turbulent
   3 more reliable
   4 more dangerous

Punctuation – conversations

A "Will you take me for a ride on your boat?" said Jose.
"Yes, you can come with Macapa and me tomorrow," replied Paco.
"Where will we be going?" he asked.
"We will take this fruit to market," said Paco.
"Thank you Paco, that will be great!" said the boy excitedly.

Spelling – *tion* suffix

A 1 (Individual work.)
   2 (Individual work.)

B 1 relation
   2 operation
   3 emotion/sensation
   4 creation
   5 education
   6 imagination
   7 invitation
   8 examination

Quiz – rhyming words

1 know = flow
2 buy = fry
3 come = some
4 said = red/read

See also: **p.98**, **Development** notes.

Nelson SKILLS BOOK 3
Unit 11
ENGLISH Pcm 1

name _____ date _____

Using adjectives to compare (1)

A Underline the correct word in these sentences.

1 The weather today is (best, better) than the weather was yesterday.

2 It is (most important, more important) that the weather is better today as we are having our fair.

3 Our school fair will be (big, bigger) this year than last year.

4 I think our fair is (most popular, more popular) than my brother's school fair.

5 Sue's fancy dress is (prettier, more pretty) than Vicky's dress.

B Choose a word or words to fill the gap in each sentence. The word in brackets will help you.

1 The judge said it was a _____ job to judge the model exhibition this year than last year. (difficult)

2 He said my model was _____ than Ravi's. (accurate)

3 Ravi's model was _____ than mine. (large)

4 Mum thought Justin's doll was _____ than Lisa's doll. (beautiful)

5 Our teacher said our model exhibition was _____ than the tombola stall. (popular)

Published by Thomas Nelson and Sons Ltd 1995   Nelson English © John Jackman and Wendy Wren 1995.

Unit 11

Using the suffix *tion*

This suffix, added to a word, usually means *the act of*.

A Select words from the box that best fill the gaps in these sentences.

| celebration | concentration | demonstration |
| competition | selection | invitation |

1 Caroline has entered a dancing _____ .

2 She will have to perform a _____ of her favourite dances.

3 An _____ has been sent to her parents to come to watch.

4 If she wins her family will have a big _____ .

5 She must keep her _____ if she is to perform well.

6 Caroline won, so she was asked to give a _____ to all the parents.

B Add the suffix **tion** to form a new word from each of these words. (Remember to drop the final *e* before adding the suffix.)

1 concentrate _____   2 celebrate _____

3 educate _____   4 situate _____

5 relate _____   6 rotate _____

7 add _____   8 create _____

9 operate _____   10 inspect _____

Skills Unit 11a

Skills Book Aims:

1 To introduce superlative forms of longer adjectives.

2 To practise noun/verb agreement.

3 To practise the *ness* suffix.

4 To review the concept of root words.

Caves and underground rivers

Teaching notes

Stimulus	diagrammatic cut-away; text and labels	This subject lends itself to large-scale wire/papier-mâché work, constructing caves with all their key characteristics.
Comprehension	cloze; literal; inferential	See general note in introduction, page 5.
Vocabulary	superlatives	**Pcm 1** provides opportunities to support the work on superlative forms, including the use of *most*.
Punctuation/ Grammar	plural verbs	Children are often fascinated by the contrasting way in which plurals are formed by nouns and verbs. **Pcm 2** demonstrates and gives opportunities to practise this.
Spelling	*ness* suffix	Collect words with this suffix. Perhaps make a large class picture of the Loch Ness Monster as a focus for this work.
Quiz	word trees	Each child in a group might take a different root word which is then illustrated. The root word is drawn on the root of a diagrammatic tree, with the derived words each forming a branch of the tree. The individual pictures can be displayed together to good effect as a frieze.

Answers

Comprehension

A 1 limestone
   2 stalactites
   3 stalagmites
   4 potholes

B 1 There are so many caves in limestone rock because, although it is a strong, tough rock, limestone slowly dissolves in water. The water that seeps through the rock carries tiny amounts of limestone away, leaving gaps that slowly grow bigger, and we call these big gaps caves.
   2 Stalactites are formed from limestone deposits in water dripping from the roof of a cave over thousands of years.
   3 A pothole is a cave entrance made by a gap in the rock that is big enough to 'swallow' a river.
   4 Opinion: I think people want to explore caves because:
(they want to know what has happened to a river so they follow it through the caves to find out where it goes.
the limestone shapes inside caves are magnificent.
they want to see what is happening to the rock, in case of subsidence.
of the thrill and excitement of exploring the unknown.)

Vocabulary – superlatives

A busy = busiest
    heavy = heaviest
    dirty = dirtiest
    mighty = mightiest
    noisy = noisiest
    pretty = prettiest
    dusty = dustiest
    lively = liveliest
    furry = furriest
    lovely = loveliest

B 1 most beautiful
   2 deepest
   3 most awkward
   4 highest

Grammar – plural verbs

A 1 wear
   2 run
   3 crawl
   4 hear

B 1 is
   2 were
   3 was
   4 were

Spelling – *ness* suffix

A 1 weakness
   2 thoughtfulness
   3 dryness
   4 kindness

B 1 happiness
   2 emptiness
   3 heaviness
   4 nastiness
   5 business

Quiz – word trees

    (Individual work.)

See also: **p.98**, Development notes.

Using adjectives to compare (2)

A Underline the correct word in these sentences.

1 It was the (busiest, busier) day of our holidays.

2 We went on the (longer, longest) walk I have ever done.

3 Gran took us to the (biggest, bigger) funfair I've seen.

4 The big dipper was the (most frightening, more frightening) ride I have seen.

5 Toby thought the sky diver was the (most exciting, more exciting) ride at the funfair.

B Underline the correct form of the adjective in each of these sentences.

1 Toby's candyfloss was (bigger, biggest) than mine.

2 He certainly finished up with a (stickier, stickiest) face!

3 Gran said he was probably the (stickier, stickiest) boy at the fair!

4 Toby said he would show me the (most terrifying, more terrifying) ride.

5 He was right. The ghost train was the (more horrible, most horrible) ride I have ever been on!

Nelson English — SKILLS BOOK 3 — **Unit 11a** — Pcm 2

name _____ date _____

Making nouns and verbs match

Draw a neat circle round the correct verb, and write **singular** or **plural** to show that the main noun or pronoun (the subject) and the verb match. The first one is done to help you.

1. Cows ((eat,) eats) grass in summer.   *plural*
2. Each cow (eat, eats) for most of the day. _____
3. The farmer (take, takes) them to be milked. _____
4. A few cows (is, are) left in the field. _____
5. He (know, knows) they don't have much milk. _____
6. Some (start, starts) to run to the shed. _____
7. The farmer (slow, slows) them down. _____
8. He (is, are) anxious they don't hurt themselves. _____
9. The children (come, comes) to watch the milking. _____
10. They all (want, wants) to help feed the calves. _____
11. Joanne (drop, drops) the bottle. _____
12. It (smash, smashes) on the ground. _____
13. She (pick, picks) up the pieces. _____
14. The farmer (smile, smiles) and gives her another one. _____
15. At the end of the day the children all (thank, thanks) the farmer. _____

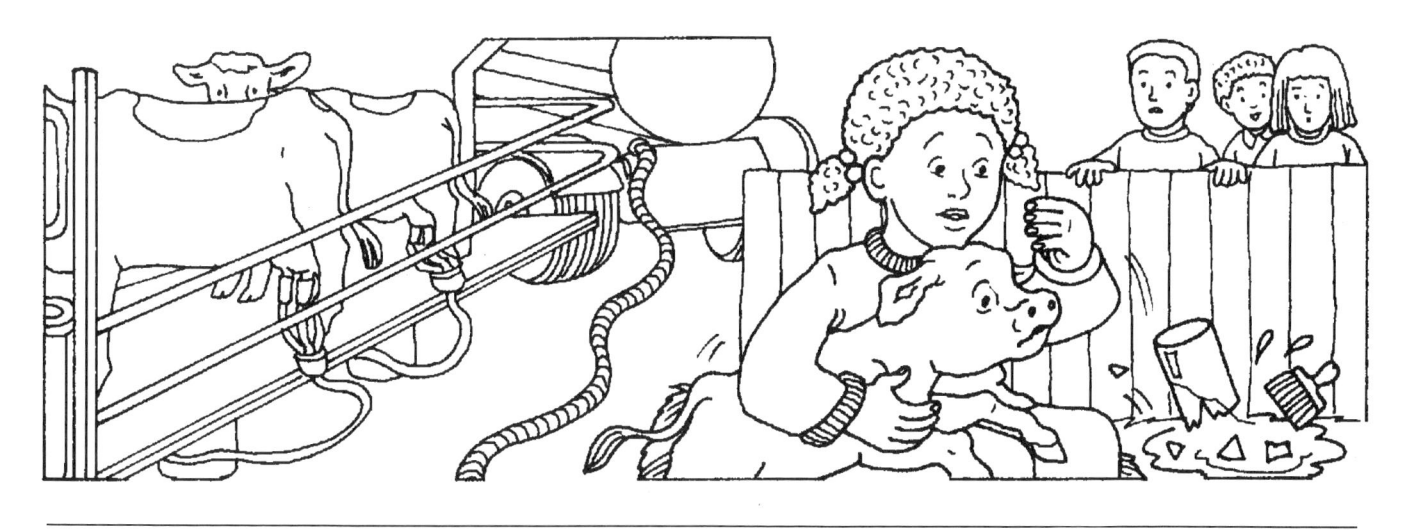

Published by Thomas Nelson and Sons Ltd 1995   Nelson English © John Jackman and Wendy Wren 1995.

Skills Unit 12

Skills Book Aims:

1 To introduce irregular adjectives.
2 To introduce auxiliary (helper) verbs.
3 To practise the *age* spelling pattern.

Fascinating body facts

Teaching notes

Stimulus	captioned illustrations	The starting point is provided for researching, collecting and displaying a host of similar fascinating facts about the human body and its performance.
Comprehension	cloze; literal; inferential	See general note in introduction, page 5.
Vocabulary	irregular adjectives	Having covered regular comparative and superlative forms in Units 11 and 11a, this unit introduces the irregular forms. The work may be extended by giving a short cloze exercise which mixes the material from all three units.
Punctuation/ Grammar	auxiliary verbs	Whilst auxiliary verbs have been introduced before, now they are being specified as such, and described as *helper* verbs. **Pcm 1** gives additional practice opportunities for *was* and *were*.
Spelling	*age* pattern	Some children are helped to recall these spellings if the *age* words are displayed around an evocative photograph or a pleasing, cheerful drawing of an elderly person. This can either be an individual task or part of a collective English work presentation.
Quiz	word selection	This can be revisited from time to time as a whole class oral/written activity, either as a 'warming-up' or as a short finishing-off item at the end of a session.

Answers

Comprehension

A 1 70
    2 Madras (a monk)
    3 Pauline Musters
    4 faster

B 1 An elephant's heart beats more slowly than a human's.
    2 (Answer will depend on whether the child is right- or left-handed.)
    3 (Opinion.)
    4 (Opinion.)

Vocabulary – irregular adjective forms

A 1 most
    2 less, least
    3 bad, worse
    4 worst

B small, smaller, smallest
    big, bigger, biggest
    pretty, prettier, prettiest
    funny, funnier, funniest
    beautiful, more beautiful, most beautiful
    fat, fatter, fattest
    terrible, more terrible, most terrible
    frightening, more frightening, most frightening
    bad, worse, worst
    little, less, least

Grammar – auxiliary verbs

A 1 have
    2 can
    3 should/can
    4 could/can
    5 has/should/could/can

B (Individual work.)

Spelling – *age* pattern

A (Individual work.)

Quiz – word selection

1 water
2 ankle
3 hair
4 duck
5 fingers
6 elbow

See also: **p.100**, **Development** notes.

Spotting auxiliary verbs

Main verbs (doing words) in a sentence sometimes need an **auxiliary** (or helper) verb.

A Draw a red line under the main verb in each sentence, and a blue line under each auxiliary verb.

1 We had run home from school.

2 Dad was sad.

3 He had lost his job.

4 We were going to cheer him up.

5 He has looked miserable lately.

6 It was snowing.

7 "We will make Dad smile tonight."

8 "You have arrived home early."

9 We had made a sledge at school.

10 "You have built that very well."

11 "We are going out with the sledge. Will you come?"

12 "Yes, I will come."

13 "We will sit on the sledge together."

14 We all had fun.

15 Dad was happy.

Skills Unit 13

Skills Book Aims:

1. To introduce alliteration.
2. To extend earlier work on synonyms.
3. To give opportunities for editing.
4. To practise spelling words which end with *le*, *el* and *al*.
5. To give activities involving wordplay.

Newspapers

Teaching notes

Stimulus	graph; cartoon; pictures	An extension to the activity suggested would be to compare different children's graphs of their results from the same newspaper. Discuss the degree of variation, and the extent of similarity in the results. Much of the work in this unit would benefit from being allied to the production of a class newspaper. This could be produced in a form which might enable it to be distributed to a wider audience. Local newspapers often welcome visits from school parties. The analysis from which the figures for letter frequency have been taken was first published in *The Guardian*.
Comprehension	cloze; literal; inferential	See general note in introduction, page 5.
Vocabulary	alliteration; synonyms	Provide a number of short articles from which the headlines have been removed. Invite the children to compete to create the wittiest and/or most effective alliterative headlines. Enriching children's written work through effective vocabulary choices is closely linked to appreciating the concept of synonyms. **Pcm 1** offers additional activities to this end.
Punctuation/ Grammar	editing	Ample opportunities for editing will be available if a class newspaper is launched. **Pcm 2** provides a simulated exercise.
Spelling	*le*, *el* and *al* endings	Encourage the use of dictionaries for part **C**. Every opportunity should be taken to point the children towards using dictionaries to check both spellings and definitions at this stage. For reasons of potential differentiation of task between different children, it can be helpful to have dictionaries available offering a range of levels of sophistication.
Quiz	word jokes	There will be little difficulty in recruiting cartoonists for a class newspaper; however, encourage jokes/cartoons which depend on a play on words.

Answers

Comprehension

A 1 E
  2 T
  3 broadsheet
  4 (Opinion.)

B 1 (Individual research.)
  2 (Opinion.)
  3 (Opinion.)
  4 (Opinion: Most newspaper headlines are very short so they will attract our attention and make us want to buy and read the newspaper. Most newspaper headlines are very short so they will be catchy and will leave space for the news articles to which they refer.)

Vocabulary – alliteration

A (Individual work.)

Vocabulary – synonyms

A 1 vacant = empty
  2 concern = worry
  3 completed = made
  4 adjacent = nearby
  5 observe = watch
  6 apprehended = arrested
  7 purchase = buy
  8 comprehend = understand

Punctuation – editing

What a shock.
I was walking home when I saw a great flash (in a nearby house).
"Help! Help me!" I heard an old lady cry from (her) window, so I dashed across (to her house) and got the ladder that was (lying) by the fence.
"Stay there!" I screamed.
"Please be quick," she called (back).
I just pulled her out (of the burning house) as the fire engine (arrived).
"Cor! That was a close thing," said (a) firefighter.
"Well done! We will make you a firefighter any day," said the Fire Chief.

Spelling – *le*, *el* and *al* endings

A (Individual research.)
B (Individual work.)
C table, kettle, tunnel, canal, barrel, whistle, actual, camel, trouble, handle, tinsel, uncle, castle, usual, arrival, angle, angel, tickle, bible, feel, triangle.

Quiz – word jokes

(Individual work.)

See also: **p.101–104**, Development notes.

Nelson English — SKILLS BOOK 3, Unit 13, Pcm 1

name _____ date _____

More synonyms

A Write one synonym for each word below. Then write *another* synonym in a sentence. The first is done to help you.

1 small   __tiny__

    Their new puppy is very little.

2 enormous _____

3 walk _____

4 happy _____

5 shop _____

B Circle the word in the sentence and the word in brackets which are synonyms.

1 Dad said he built things.   (constructed   showed   painted)

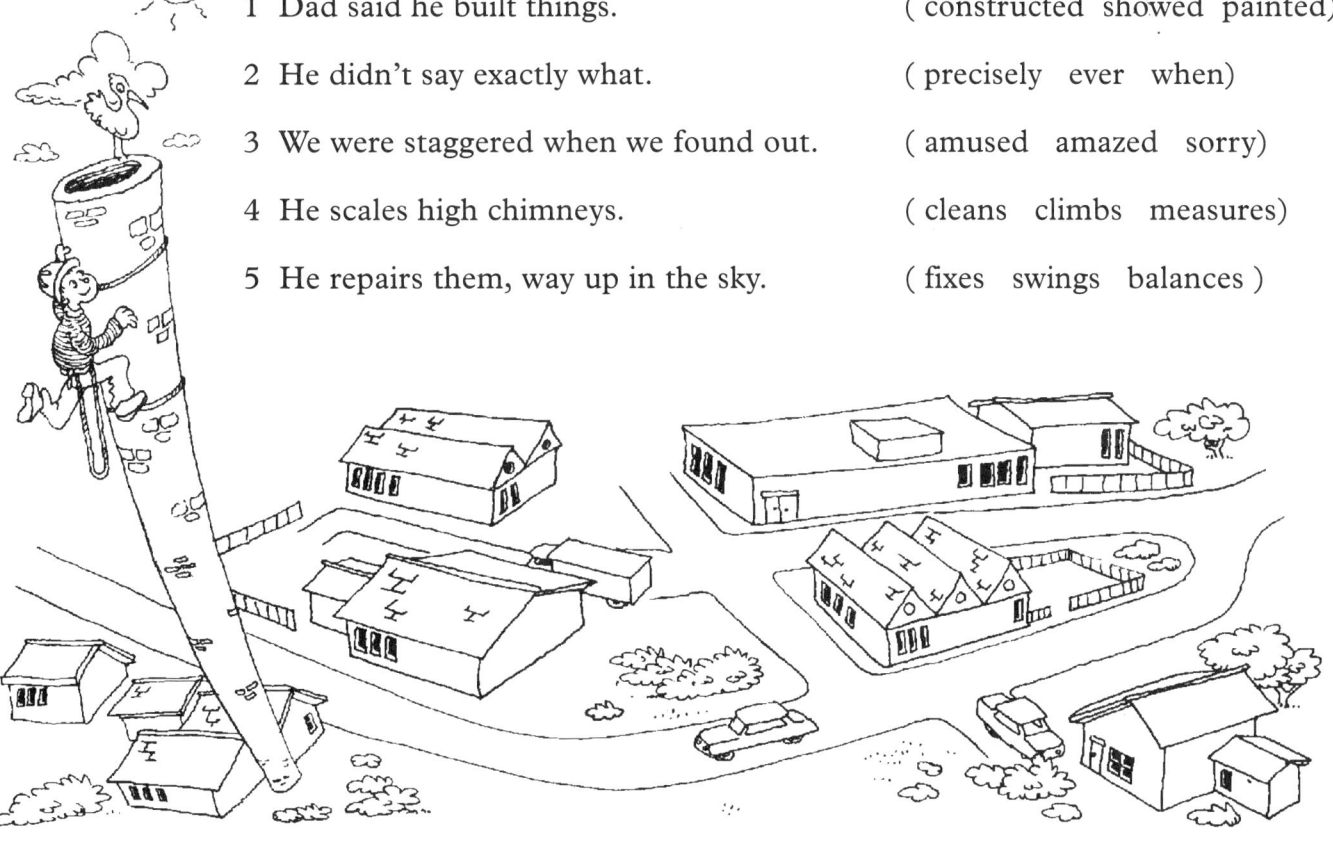

2 He didn't say exactly what.   (precisely   ever   when)

3 We were staggered when we found out.   (amused   amazed   sorry)

4 He scales high chimneys.   (cleans   climbs   measures)

5 He repairs them, way up in the sky.   (fixes   swings   balances)

Published by Thomas Nelson and Sons Ltd 1995   Nelson English © John Jackman and Wendy Wren 1995.

Editing

You are a sub-editor working for the Chatterthorpe Chronicle. The editor has asked you to edit this article for next week's issue. Re-write it, correcting spellings and punctuation. Before you start think how you can make it more interesting and exciting for your readers. Think carefully about the words you might use.

Chatterthorpe Primary Wins the Cup

Their was grate excitement on saterday. The local team got threw to the final of the six-a-side competition when James porter got a nice goal in the last seconds off the match before the finals with st christophers school, he got the ball and ran and ran and ran in and out and in and out of the players in the other team. He got a really good goal.

In the final james did it again and got another nice goal. Everyone watching got really excited especially when peasdown school got a goal back, but then James got another goal and chatterthorpe won.

Skills Unit 14

Skills Book Aims:

1 To introduce thesauruses.

2 To introduce future tense, and revise auxiliary verbs.

3 To practise the *ght* spelling pattern.

4 To encourage alternatives to *said*.

Moon – in the future

Teaching notes

Stimulus	letter; photograph	Most children are fascinated by the possibilities offered by space exploration. This unit has been devised to encourage personal/imaginative writing as an extension to the skills work presented in this topic.
Comprehension	cloze; literal; inferential	See general note in introduction, page 5.
Vocabulary	using a thesaurus	If possible have a range of thesauruses available, demonstrating different styles of arrangement. Thesaurus skills are not easily mastered by some children, so group or individual support may be necessary. **Pcm 1c** gives additional activities: **pcm 1a** and **pcm 1b** are thesaurus pages for use with **pcm 1c**. (**Note:** The exercises in the **pupils' book** can all be undertaken with reference to the sample page in the unit.)
Punctuation/ Grammar	future tense	**Pcm 2** gives extra practice if required.
Spelling	*ght* pattern	As all teachers will recognise, this is one of the spelling 'classics', and well worth additional/personalised support as appropriate.
Quiz	*said* words	The activity requires the children to find ten alternatives to using *said*. Pool the groups' results and make a more or less permanent list available for reference as a wall chart, to encourage a widening use of these words in the children's everyday writing.

Answers

Comprehension

A 1 Moon
   2 roof
   3 street
   4 weightless

B 1 Tim and Kate went on holiday in the year 2095.
   2 They travelled to the Moon on the Moonferry.
   3 (Opinion.)
   4 (Opinion.)

Vocabulary – using a thesaurus

A 1 exciting = thrilling, stirring, startling, arousing, hair-raising, stimulating.
   2 expensive = dear, costly, excessive, exorbitant, extortionate.
   3 fall = drop, sink, descend, plummet.
   4 facts = information, data.

B 2 expensive: *synonym* = dear, costly, unreasonable, excessive, exorbitant, extortionate; *antonym* = cheap, inexpensive
   3 ever: *synonym* = always, forever, evermore, continually, repeatedly, perpetually; *antonym* = never.
   4 fact: *synonym* = truth, information, reality, data, certainty, activity; *antonym* = fiction.
   5 fade: *synonym* = disappear, vanish, wither, blanch, pale, decline; *antonym* = last.

Grammar – future tense

A 1 shall
   2 will
   3 will
   4 will
   5 will
   6 shall

B 1 I will do it.
   2 You shall go to bed when I ask.

Spelling – *ght* pattern

A 1 (Individual research.)
   2 (Individual work.)

B 1 thought
   2 brought
   3 caught
   4 taught, daughter
   5 bright light

Quiz – *said* words

   (Individual work.)

See also: **p.105**, **Development** notes.

Nelson English — SKILLS BOOK 3, Unit 14, Pcm 1a

name _____ date _____

Using a thesaurus

Here is a copy of page 32 of *The Nelson Concise Thesaurus*.

---

785 useful   **792** view

785 useful
manipulate
useful
useless
[see 785]

785
useful
(useless)
helpful
handy
convenient
worthwhile
effective
utilitarian
usefulness
[see 784]

786
usual
(exceptional)
ordinary
common
familiar
normal
typical
unremarkable
usually
[see 132]

787
vacant
(occupied)
empty
unoccupied
abandoned
uninhabited
deserted
void
vacancy
vacancies
[see 68, 196]

788
valuable
(worthless)
costly
expensive
rare
special
precious
priceless
value
[see 833]

789
various
several
many
different
assorted

dissimilar
variegated
[see 379]

790
vehicle
coach
carriage
wagon
automobile
conveyance
transporter
[see 94]

791
very
(slightly)
quite
highly
remarkably
extremely
exceedingly
unequivocally

792
view
sight
scene

contd.

Using a thesaurus

Here is a copy of page 99 of *The Nelson Concise Thesaurus*.

| 250 germ | | 257 go |

250
germ
bug
microbe
bacteria
virus
bacillus
micro-organism

251
get
(lose)
earn
receive
obtain
bring
fetch
acquire
getting
got
[see 2, 244, 438, 536, 539, 717]

252
gift
(forfeit)
present
favour
grant
offering
donation
bequest
[see 502]

253
girl
(boy)
lass
maiden
damsel
female
woman
young lady

254
give
(take)
offer
afford
supply
spare
donate
contribute
gave

255
glad
(sorry)
happy
pleased
delighted
thrilled
contented
satisfied
gladness
gladly
[see 108, 248, 270]

256
glass
beaker
crystal
tumbler
wineglass
goblet
chalice

257
go
(come)
move
walk
travel
set out
leave
depart
going
gone
went
[see 409]

Unit 14

Nelson SKILLS BOOK 3
ENGLISH Pcm 1c

name _____ date _____

Using a thesaurus

A Look carefully at your photocopies of the thesaurus pages. Use the pages to help you to answer these questions.

1 What is the antonym of each of these words?

girl	_____	give	_____
useful	_____	vacant	_____
get	_____	go	_____
very	_____	valuable	_____
glad	_____	gift	_____
usual	_____		

2 Write three synonyms for each of these words.

get	_____	_____	_____
go	_____	_____	_____
glad	_____	_____	_____
valuable	_____	_____	_____
very	_____	_____	_____
useful	_____	_____	_____

B Replace each word printed in bold type with a synonym.

1 Grandad said his new electric screwdriver would be very **useful** / _____ .

2 There were **various** / _____ jobs he could use it for.

3 He was surprised to **get** / _____ it.

4 We told him it was really an early birthday **gift** / _____ .

5 Grandad seemed **very** / _____ pleased.

6 He said he was **glad** / _____ to have it.

7 Grandad thought it was **valuable** / _____ too.

8 We were happy that we had thought to **give** / _____ him this gift.

Future tense

We often need to use an auxiliary (helper) verb with the main verb when writing about something which will happen in the future.

A Russell and Amy are planning their holiday. Fill in the gaps with verbs in the future tense.

1 "I ___will need___ lots of clothes," said Amy.

2 "That _____ your bag heavy to carry," replied Russell.

3 "We _____ next to each other on the coach," suggested Russell.

4 "You are saying that because you know I _____ sweets before we get on the coach," Amy laughed.

5 "Mum _____ you to catch the coach," said Dad.

6 "Unfortunately I _____ at work, so can't come to wave you off," he added.

B These sentences tell of something that happened in the past. Rewrite each verb to change the event to a time in the future.

1 Anna **phoned** the travel agent. _____

2 They **sent** her information about Spain. _____

3 She **read** the brochures. _____

4 She **booked** her trip. _____

5 She **had** a great time. _____

6 Buzzzz! Her alarm clock **woke** her for school. _____

Skills Unit 14a

Skills Book Aims:

1. To extend the concept of gender words to *common* and *neuter*.
2. To introduce syllables.
3. To revise and extend adverbs.
4. To practise the *dge* spelling pattern.
5. To revisit popular homophones.

Earth

Teaching notes

Stimulus	modern poetry; pictures	Make a collection/class anthology of space poems. The poem makes reference to an eclipse. This can provide an opportunity for extending the work into an understanding of the relative arrangements/orbits of Earth, our moon, the other planets and the Sun. Note that the poem erroneously makes reference to 'light years' as a measurement of time. Discuss light years being a measurement of distance, challenging pupils to research and define the term.
Comprehension	cloze; literal; inferential	See general note in introduction, page 5.
Vocabulary	gender words; syllables	The terms *male* and *female*, refined to *masculine* and *feminine*, and *common* and *neuter* are introduced. The concept of syllables is introduced and additional work is available on **pcm 1**.
Punctuation/ Grammar	adverbs	Well-chosen adverbs bring greater colour and depth to children's writing, so the awareness of this potential, and practising it, can be beneficial and offer immediate rewards in many cases. **Pcm 2** provides further support exercises.
Spelling	*dge* pattern	The *age* pattern was practised in Unit 12, and it might be helpful to refer back to this. This pattern, and the rule about when to use the *silent d*, extends that work.
Quiz	homophones	Some children might be able to produce a similar passage, including as many homophones as they can. This could then be set as a quick exercise for others in the class.

Answers

Comprehension

A 1 Sun
2 one
3 eight
4 collapse

B 1 It takes the Earth a day and a night to spin once on its axis.
2 The Moon sometimes comes between the Earth and the Sun.
3 The Earth's orbit takes it around the Sun.
4 Individual answers.

Vocabulary – gender words

A **feminine:** mother, her, princess, cow
masculine: father, him, bull, policeman, he
common: parents, teacher, they, singer, calf, you
neuter: space, Earth, Sun, cowshed, field

B (Individual research.)

C grandfather, king, duke, uncle, cock, him, he, man, monk, bull.

Vocabulary – syllables

A 1 vill/age
2 or/bit
3 some/thing
4 shi/ning
5 o/cean
6 of/ten
7 pic/ture

B 1 *Options include:* I, am, your, the, one, that, gave, you, birth, a, green, spot, clean, that's, known, as, Earth, My, on, round, the, Sun, through, space, no, trace, Each, lap, means, year, gone, spin, once, day, and, right, say, lean, way, I'm, to, think, they're, right, have, Moon, comes, me, for, time, know, Plunged, in, Stars, eight, ask, who, put, them, place, when, did, it, why, whole, Scheme, will, there's, can, do, not, much, go, light, years, or, so, Are.

2 *Options include:* planet, Mother, orbit, never, changes, journey, circling, leaving, upon, axis, every, inclined, sometimes, between, other, planets, arranged, happen, Experts, collapse, nothing, mankind, longer, billion, going, worry.

3 *Options include:* favourite, Observers, obscurity, consider.

See also: **p.105**, **Development** notes.

Nelson English — SKILLS BOOK 3 — Unit 14a — Pcm 1

name _____ date _____

Syllables

A *syllable* is a part of a word that can be said by itself.

A Fill in the numbers in this chart. Two have been done to help you.

	Number of vowel letters	Number of vowel sounds	Number of syllables
1 hot	1	1	1
2 fast			
3 sheep			
4 spoon			
5 fly			
6 supper			
7 cattle			
8 invisible			
9 prickly			
10 exclamation			
11 imagination	6	5	5
12 sleepily			
13 pavement			
14 motionless			

B Put a **/** between the syllables in each of these words.

1 under
2 inspect
3 because
4 mountain
5 orchestra
6 untidy
7 tortoise
8 hippopotamus

Nelson English — Skills Book 3, Unit 14a, Pcm 2

name _____ date _____

Adverbs

An *adverb* tells us *how*, *when* or *where* the action of a verb takes place.

A In each of these sentences, underline the adverb and circle the verb it is describing. Then write *how*, *when* or *where* next to the sentence to show what the adverb tells us.

1 The children crept quietly towards the door. _____

2 Krishna opened it carefully. _____

3 They stood silently, looking into the darkness. _____

4 Then Indira stepped forward and peered in. _____

5 Suddenly a large bat flew past them. _____

6 Immediately they heard a huge crash. _____

7 "Let's get away from here fast," said Krishna. _____

8 They ran as swiftly as their legs would take them. _____

B Use the adverbs in the box to fill the gaps in these sentences.

| Softly | never | Eventually | slowly |

1 _____ the two stopped running.

2 They _____ turned to look back at the old ruin.

3 _____ Indira whispered to her brother.

4 "I'll _____ go there again!"

Published by Thomas Nelson and Sons Ltd 1995

Nelson English © John Jackman and Wendy Wren 1995.

Skills Book
Check-up 1 Answers

Vocabulary

A Mum **received** a **beautiful**, new coat for Christmas and Dad **was given** a tool set. "You are **kind**," said Mum, as I **handed** her my present from under the tree. "What's inside?" asked Dad, looking at the **pretty** paper. "You **have** to wait and see," I whispered. "Christmas is a **jolly** time," said Gran with a grin.

B 2 unwrap
    3 incomplete
    4 distrust
    5 impossible
    6 disappear

Punctuation

A 1 "<u>You have eaten too much</u>," laughed Dad.
    2 "<u>Oh no I haven't</u>," said Kim, "<u>but I can't eat anything else!</u>"

B "So you won't want any pudding then?" asked mum.
    "Well, I'll squeeze in just a little piece," said Kim.

C 1 My brother had a bike, a helmet, a football, a Lego set and a computer game for Christmas.
    2 Mum and Dad gave me a pretty, white, fluffy, cuddly kitten.
    3 It was Christmas Eve, the snow was falling and I just knew we were going to have the best Christmas ever.

Grammar

A 1 he = James
    2 you = James
    3 he = Santa Claus
    4 you = James
    5 he = Santa Claus
    6 you = James
    7 I = James
    8 she = Grandma
    9 me = James

B Yesterday we had a party and lots of my friends were at my flat. We played games and made lots of noise, but nobody minded because it was New Year's Day.

Spelling

A 1 halves
    2 knives
    3 wives
    4 shelves

B 1 watch
    2 match
    3 catch
    4 write
    5 hear
    6 bear

Skills Book
Check-up 2 Answers

Vocabulary

A 1 Indian
    2 African
    3 Canadian
    4 Welsh
    5 Spanish
    6 French

B 1 Sparrow; the others are four-legged and cannot fly.
    2 Kangaroo; the others are big cats.
    3 Siamese (cat); the others are breeds of dog.

C 1 jump
    2 attractive
    3 savage

D 1 almost
    2 although
    3 beautiful

Punctuation

A Last week Mr Purewal came to talk to our class at Caversham Primary School. He told us about some of the animals in Pakistan and India, including tigers, elephants, vultures, cobras and kraits.
    Laura asked, "What is the rarest animal in India?"
    "I can't be sure," replied Mr Purewal, "but there are now fewer than forty white tigers."
    We all enjoyed his really interesting talk and our teacher, Mrs Stephens, thanked him and asked him to come again soon. He said he would.

Grammar

A 1 The wolf's jaw is powerful (yet/but) it can pick up an egg without cracking it.
    2 The lioness had two cubs this year (but/yet/although) she only had one cub last year.
    3 The bee-keeper wears protective clothing (as/because/since) he doesn't want to be stung.
    4 The seal searched and searched along the beach (until/and) she found her lost pup.

B 1 ran
    2 jumped
    3 bit
    4 found
    5 said
    6 fell
    7 threw
    8 came
    9 swam
    10 walked
    11 danced
    12 stole

C 1 Jane's kitten meowed.
    2 The two kittens' mother.
    3 A lion's head appeared.
    4 Look at Delroy's hamster.
    5 Surinder's pony was grazing.
    6 The three bears growled.

Spelling

A 1 field
    2 receive
    3 chief
    4 piece
    5 ceiling
    6 thief
    7 weird
    8 pier

B 1 cockatoos
    2 bamboo (bamboos is correct but rarely used)
    3 pianos
    4 mottoes
    5 volcanoes
    6 cellos
    7 potatoes
    8 tomatoes
    9 echoes
    10 photos
    11 solos
    12 radios

C 1 mice
    2 face
    3 race
    4 since
    5 cosy
    6 chance
    7 palace
    8 mist
    9 dance
    10 noise
    11 fierce
    12 horse

Skills Book Check-up 3 Answers

A 1 We're
   2 were
   3 Where
   4 Where
   5 We're
   6 where we're

C 2 hot = hotter, hottest
   3 cold = colder, coldest
   4 sunny = sunnier, sunniest
   5 beautiful = more beautiful, most beautiful
   6 dangerous = more dangerous, most dangerous
   7 nervous = more nervous, most nervous
   8 safe = safer, safest
   9 difficult = more difficult, most difficult
   10 dusty = dustier, dustiest
   11 warm = warmer, warmest

Punctuation

"Do you remember when we were young and played on this beach, George?" asked Mary.

"I certainly do, my dear," replied the old gentleman as he watched the children.

"In our day we didn't have all these wonderful toys and games," said Mary, "but we still had fun, didn't we?"

"We certainly did," said George wistfully.

Grammar

A 1 who
   2 which
   3 which
   4 which
   5 who

B 1 were
   2 is
   3 was
   4 are
   5 is
   6 were
   7 were
   8 were
   9 was
   10 was

Spelling

A 2 comfortable
   3 lovable
   4 sensible
   5 responsible
   6 usable
   7 reasonable
   8 forcible
   9 valuable
   10 curable
   11 changeable

B 1 education
   2 relation
   3 operation
   4 observation
   5 situation
   6 regulation
   7 appreciation
   8 dictation

C (Answers depend on classroom dictionaries.)

D 1 sadness
   2 kindness
   3 laziness
   4 ugliness
   5 happiness
   6 sickness
   7 thoughtfulness
   8 emptiness
   9 nastiness
   10 business
   11 helpfulness
   12 prettiness

Skills Book Check-up 4 Answers

Vocabulary

A small, smaller, smallest
   busy, busier, busiest
   good, better, best
   many, more, most
   bad, worse, worst
   happy, happier, happiest
   miserable, more miserable, most miserable
   beautiful, more beautiful, most beautiful
   interesting, more interesting, most interesting

B 2 fast: *antonym* = slow; *synonym* = quick, rapid
   3 tiny: *antonym* = huge, big, massive, vast; *synonym* = small, slight
   4 happy: *antonym* = sad, miserable, gloomy; *synonym* = merry, jolly, cheerful
   5 fracture: *antonym* = mend, fix, repair; *synonym* = break
   6 inside: *antonym* = outside; *synonym* = within

C 2 father = masculine
   3 hen = feminine
   4 person = common
   5 cabbage = neuter
   6 princess = feminine
   7 Moon = neuter
   8 children = common
   9 grandfather = masculine
   10 cattle = common

D (Individual answers.)

Punctuation

A 1 Bob and Vicky ran home to see their Uncle Brian from Australia.
   2 Bill, Delroy, Winston and Gemma were already there.
   3 "It is certainly good to see you kids," said Uncle Brian.
   4 "Your cousins David, Joy and Tim send you their love," he said.
   5 "Do you want to see how I throw a boomerang?" asked their uncle.
   6 "Yes, please!" shouted the children.
   7 "Oh dear me!" exclaimed Gran. "Do be careful."
   8 Crash! went the glass in the greenhouse.

B (Individual answers.)

Grammar

A 1 will
   2 shall
   3 shall
   4 will
   5 will
   6 will
   7 will

B 2 today = present
   3 now = present
   4 next Christmas = future
   5 tomorrow = future
   6 a fortnight ago = past
   7 the day before yesterday = past
   8 last century = past
   9 in the year 2000 = future
   10 this minute = present
   11 my next birthday = future
   12 when I was a baby = past

C 1 I ate my breakfast.
   2 They felt hungry.
   3 The fox crept through the reeds towards the heron.
   4 I hated going to the dentist.

D (Individual answers.)

E 1 quickly
   2 truthfully
   3 early
   4 today
   5 outside
   6 away

F (Individual answers.)

Spelling

A 1 capital
   2 Tunnel
   3 garage
   4 daughter
   5 towel

Development Book 3 Scope and Sequence

Unit	Stimulus	Comprehension	Writing	Working with words
1 A Winter's tale	famous painting; planning sheet; story beginnings; pictures	literal – painting; inferential – painting; literal – story beginnings	story writing – making a plan; filling in a planning sheet; analysing/writing story beginnings	choosing the right words
2 Footprints in the snow	factual texts	literal – factual texts; inferential – factual texts	fact/opinion – which is which?; sentence writing	*snow* words
3 Tudor and Stuart theatre	factual text; annotated diagram; narrative; playscript; illustrations	literal – text; inferential – text; literal – diagram	playscripts; research – dictionary	theatre words
4 Tudor and Stuart beliefs	factual text; playscript; pictures	literal – text; inferential – text	magic spells; rhyming words; descriptive; research – dictionary	modern poetry – homophones
5 Gale warning!	factual text; chart; pictures; weather report; photographs	literal – chart; literal – pictures	weather report; descriptive; letter writing	choosing the right words
6 India	encyclopedia entries; travel brochure; photographs	literal – atlas, info. books, dictionary, encyclopedia; literal – travel brochure; looking at persuasive writing	travel brochure articles; persuasive/dissuasive	phrases to persuade/dissuade
7 An Indian childhood	autobiography; time lines; pictures	literal – text	time line; personal/autobiography; letter writing	personal details
8 Remember, remember…	poetry; acrostics; instructions; pictures	literal – poetry; inferential – poetry	acrostics; shape poetry; analysing instructions; posters; research – encyclopedia and info. books; making notes	similes
9 Bushfire	narrative text; information on story endings; pictures; rock painting	literal – narrative; inferential – narrative; literal – picture; inferential – picture	planning a story – endings; finishing the story; descriptive; list of adjectives and adverbs	*fire* words

77

Development Book 3 **Scope and Sequence** continued

Unit	Stimulus	Comprehension	Writing	Working with words
10 Victorian schooldays	photographs; narrative text – classic fiction; pictures	literal – photograph; inferential – text	making notes; descriptive; personal – expressing preferences; personal/autobiography	*quad* words; *bi* words; *tri* words
11 Forests	narrative text; annotated diagram; info. on purpose and audience; pictures	literal – text; inferential – text; literal – diagram; inferential – diagram	analysing types of writing – purpose/audience; classifying types of writing	opposites with *dis*
12 Eat to live	factual text; poetry; info. on persuasive writing; pictures	literal – poetry; inferential – poetry	imaginative – feelings; pros and cons	idioms
13 Printing and writing	factual text; pictures; fact file; info. on biographies	literal – text; inferential – text	research – encyclopedia, info. books; interviews – note-taking	writers
13a Read all about it!	newspaper report; map; photograph; picture	literal – report; literal – map; inferential – photograph	newspaper reports – facts; eye-witness accounts	abbreviations
14 Earth… In the beginning	narrative – biblical text; narrative – legend; presenting information; pictures	literal – biblical text; literal – legend	purpose and audience – writing for young children; research – dictionary	complex/simple words

Development Unit 1

Development Book Aims:

1 Planning narrative writing.

2 Story beginnings.

A Winter's tale

Teaching notes

Stimulus	famous painting; planning sheet; story beginnings; pictures	**Picture study** *Hunters in the Snow* by Pieter Brueghel the Elder.
Comprehension	literal – painting; inferential – painting; literal – story beginnings	Comprehension to make children look closely at the picture and imagine how the hunters feel. Discuss how it feels to be out in the snow. Draw on the children's personal experience.

Writing	story writing – making a plan; filling in a planning sheet; analysing/ writing story beginnings	**Making a story plan**
		Recapping on components of narrative writing introduced in **Development Book 2**.
		    Pcm 1 – Story planning sheet, for the children to outline the story based on *Hunters in the Snow*.
		    Children can be given other famous paintings to devise story plans.
		Story beginnings
		A detailed look at the various uses of story beginnings. Children can look at other stories and analyse what the opening paragraphs tell them and what they have yet to find out.
		Beginning your own story
		Children can use the extracts from *Story beginnings* as models for their work.

Working with words	choosing the right words	The *What do you mean?* sentences can be expanded into story beginnings which are concerned with setting the scene.

Marking suggestion

Teachers may choose to paste photocopies of the unit answers on to cards and store these in a simple box, so the children can check their own answers, as appropriate.

Each card should be clearly labelled with the book title and unit number and title, to enable the children to find and use the correct unit answers easily.

See also: **p.25**, **Skills** notes.

Nelson English — DEVELOPMENT BOOK 3 — **Unit 1** — Pcm 1

name _____ date _____

Story Planning Sheet

1 **Title**

2 **Setting**

3 **Characters**

4 **Plot**   **Beginning**

         Middle

         End

Development Unit 2

Development Book Aims:

1 To look at the difference between fact and opinion.

Footprints in the snow

Teaching notes

Stimulus	factual texts	**Fact and opinion** The passage and following comprehension questions provide the context for work on fact and opinion.
Comprehension	literal – factual texts; inferential – factual texts	**What do we know?** This is an information section to ensure the children appreciate the difference between fact and opinion. **Pcm 1** – Fact and opinion, will give them further practice. Oral work can reinforce this – one child giving a fact about something and another expressing an opinion.
Writing	fact/opinion – which is which?; sentence writing	**The Abominable Snowman** A passage for the children to work on themselves regarding fact and opinion. This type of exercise can be done with other texts e.g. newspaper reports.
Working with words	*snow* words	Revise compound words. Can the children find the compound word in the text about The Abominable Snowman? (footprints.)

Answers

Comprehension – *Footprints in the snow*

1 "there was a heavy fall of snow".

2 The footprints were four inches long and looked as if they had been made by something with two legs and hooves.

3 (Opinion: No ordinary animal has two legs and hooves.)

4 (Individual answer.)

Comprehension – *The Abominable Snowman*

1 **Fact**
Names: Yeti, Big Foot, Kang-Mi, the Abominable Snowman.
Eric Shipton's photographs: human-like prints, 13 inches long, 8 inches wide, found in the Himalayas.
Other clues, such as teeth, have been found.
All the descriptions are about the same.

Opinion
Whether such a strange man-like creature exists.
Description: up to ten feet tall, about 300 pounds, walks upright, is very hairy.
Eric Shipton said the footprints he saw were too large to have been made by a bear.
Some people think that the creature is a big ape but many do not believe it exists at all.
The clues, such as teeth, could be those of bears, wolves or snow leopards.
It is thought that people who claim they have seen the Abominable Snowman are just imagining things.

Working with words

snowball = a ball made of snow pressed together.
snowdrift = a bank of snow blown by the wind.
snowfall = a fall of snow.
snowline = the level above which there is always snow.
snowstorm = bad weather with snow.

(Individual research.)

See also: **p.28**, **Skills** notes. 81

Fact and opinion

Look at the pictures.

It is raining. I think it will rain all night.

I buried my bone in this garden. I think it is under the tree.

What does the girl know?

_____

What does the dog know?

_____

What does the girl think?

_____

What does the dog think?

_____

We are playing a match tomorrow. I think we will win.

I have to buy bread. I think we need potatoes as well.

What does the boy know?

_____

What does the man know?

_____

What does the boy think?

_____

What does the man think?

_____

Development Unit 3

Development Book Aims:

1 To introduce playscripts.

Tudor and Stuart theatre

Teaching notes

Stimulus	factual text; annotated diagram; narrative; playscript; illustrations	**Tudor and Stuart theatre** Discuss going to see a play with the children. Most of them will have some experience of this, e.g. school play, pantomime, 'theatre in education visit'. How does their own experience differ from what they have read about?
Comprehension	literal – text; inferential – text; literal – diagram	**Setting out a playscript** As a class, ask the children to recount the story of Hansel and Gretel. They can work in groups to continue the script. Some groups can work on other well-known stories.
Writing	playscripts; research – dictionary	**Pcm 1** – Setting out a playscript. Here the children are required to translate the strip cartoon into a playscript. Can they make a strip cartoon of their own for a friend to make into a playscript? **Writing your own play** Point out that the information regarding the scene, dialogue and characters can be found in the text and illustrations. They will have to think of suitable stage directions. How might the young man's wife speak? (Angrily, peevishly, etc.) What might the young man do when his wife comes to complain? (Turn away, continue with his work, sigh, etc.)
Working with words	theatre words	Can the children think of any more words connected with the theatre? Some of them they have already met in this unit.

Answers

Comprehension

1 Examples: The actors would have had problems performing from the back of a wagon because:

i) there would not have been much space for the actors so there could not have been many actors on stage at once, which limits the dramatic possibilities;

ii) the kinds of scenes shown would have been limited by lack of space and scenery;

iii) actors must often not have been able to enter or leave the stage without being seen, which makes it harder to keep the audience's interest;

iv) the wagon may have been unstable;

v) it must often have been difficult to persuade the passing people to stop what they were doing, watch and believe in the performance, because the people would know that they were looking at the back of a wagon in their own familiar town setting, which must have made it hard for the actors to win and keep the audience's interest.

2 People that watched from the pit were called 'groundlings' because they could not afford to pay for a seat to watch the play so they stood on the ground.

3 Wealthy people who had money to spare for pleasurable activities could afford to watch from the balconies.

4 The actors would have to shout their lines or surprise their audience, with music, a loud noise or sudden entrance, exit or dramatic scene, when the audience was making a lot of noise.

5 (Individual research.)

Writing your own play

(Individual work.)

Working with words

actor	=	player on a stage, film or radio
actress	=	female player
cue	=	the last words of an actor's speech which tell the next speaker to continue
role	=	part played by an actor or actress
wings	=	sides of a stage
audience	=	people watching the play

See also: **p.31**, **Skills** notes.

Nelson
DEVELOPMENT BOOK 3
Unit 3
ENGLISH Pcm 1

name _____   date _____

Setting out a playscript

Read the picture story.

[Picture story with six panels:

Panel 1: "I think we're lost, Tom." / "No. Look at the map, Ali. We just have to follow the river."

Panel 2: "What a strange tree." / "That's on the map as well."

Panel 3: "I hope we find the treasure before it gets dark." / "So do I, Ali."

Panel 4: "Look! There's the cave!" / "Quick, we've found it."

Panel 5: "Dig here." / "Yes this is the spot."

Panel 6: "We've found it! We've found it!" / "The map was right."]

Set out the picture story as a playscript. Use the back of this sheet if you need more space.

Scene _____

Characters   **What they say**

_____   _____
_____   _____
_____   _____
_____   _____
_____   _____
_____   _____
_____   _____
_____   _____
_____   _____
_____   _____
_____   _____
_____   _____
_____   _____

Development Unit 4

Development Book Aims:

1. To continue work on playscripts.

2. To use descriptive writing to set the scene of a play.

Tudor and Stuart beliefs

Teaching notes

Stimulus	factual text; playscript; pictures	Factual text about Tudor and Stuart beliefs. Extract from *Macbeth* by William Shakespeare.
Comprehension	literal – text; inferential – text	**Tudor and Stuart beliefs** This gives the opportunity to introduce the idea that fictional writing is often a response to things that are really happening. Many stories look at real events, beliefs, etc. in an imaginative way. **Double, double, toil and trouble** One of the fictional responses to the belief in witches can be seen in the play *Macbeth*. What do the children already know about Shakespeare? What can they find out?
Writing	magic spells; rhyming words; descriptive; research – dictionary	The witches' spell gives the opportunity for group drama work. The children's own magic spells can be stuck on to black paper cauldrons for display. **Note:** regional or cultural variations in dialect and pronunciation may affect the children's perceptions of rhymes. Also, the 'visual rhymes', like stone – one and blood – good, may be listed here by some children. **Setting the scene** **Pcm 1** – Setting the scene, provides support for this writing task.
Working with words	modern poetry – homophones	Discuss homophones with the children. Make a class list on the blackboard. (See **Skills Book 3**, page 5.)

Answers

Comprehension

1. People found it easy to believe in witches because there were so many things that could not be explained by the scientific or medical knowledge of the time.

2. Examples: crop failure, accidents, food or drink going bad, people or things going missing – these are all things for which witches might be blamed.

3. Example: Putting people accused of being witches into water to prove their guilt or innocence was not a fair test because people do not want to risk drowning to 'prove' their innocence; people generally float in water because of the fat in their bodies; and women's clothes at this time – long dresses with petticoats in layers – would trap air at first and prevent sinking, but they would slowly soak up water and drag the woman down and probably cause her to drown, so whatever happened in this test, people accused of being witches would die one way or another.

Comprehension – *Double, double, toil and trouble*

1. poisoned entrails
   toad
   sweltered venom
   fillet of a fenny snake
   eye of newt
   toe of frog
   wool of bat
   tongue of dog
   adder's fork
   blind-worm's sting
   lizard's leg
   howlet's wing
   baboon's blood

2. End of line rhymes include:
   go – throw
   got – pot
   trouble – bubble
   snake – bake
   frog – dog
   sting – wing
   thumbs – comes
   Other internal rhymes include:
   Boil – toil
   Double – trouble/bubble
   locks – knocks

Working with words

1. which = what particular one?
   witch = a woman thought to have magical powers
   foul = dirty, disgusting;
   fowl = a bird, especially a domestic hen
   draft = first attempt;
   draught = a drink or dose of medicine
   tale = a story;
   tail = the back end of an animal
   hoarse = husky and rough voiced
   horse = animal used for riding and drawing loads
   flew = moved through the air;
   flue = inside part of chimney
   tied = fastened with string or rope;
   tide = the regular rise and fall of the sea
   ate = past tense of 'eat';
   eight = number which is one more than seven but one less than nine
   pair = a set of two of the same kind;
   pear = fruit
   eerie = weird, strange;
   eyrie = nest of bird of prey
   knight = a man bearing the title 'Sir';
   night = time between sunset and sunrise
   pray = speak to God;
   prey = something that is hunted

2. pair = pear
   blue = blew
   bare = bear
   stair = stare
   birth = berth

See also: **p.34**, **Skills** notes. 85

Nelson English — DEVELOPMENT BOOK 3 — Unit 4 — Pcm 1

name _____   date _____

Setting the scene

You are going to make the stage look like a witches' cave.

Underline in blue the words which describe the cave.
Underline in red the words which describe the cauldron.

welcoming   eerie   pretty   hot

dark   damp   clean   dirty

bright   cold   bubbling   black

gloomy   pleasant   steaming

Now write a description of the cave and the cauldron using the words you have underlined.

_____
_____
_____
_____
_____
_____
_____
_____
_____
_____
_____

Published by Thomas Nelson and Sons Ltd 1995   Nelson English © John Jackman and Wendy Wren 1995.

Development Unit 5

Development Book Aims:

1. To use charts conveying information.
2. To develop factual writing.

Gale warning!

Teaching notes

Stimulus	factual text; chart; pictures; weather report; photographs	Factual text about wind strength. Beaufort Scale.
Comprehension	literal – chart; literal – pictures	**Gale warning!** This gives the children the opportunity to gather information from a source other than continuous text. **Using the Beaufort Scale** The children can also use the Beaufort Scale orally in a quiz, e.g. 'Large branches are moving and there is a strong breeze. What is the force of the wind?' 'The wind is force 11. How many mph is it travelling?' Ask the children to listen to weather forecasts on television or radio taking particular notice of the comments about the wind.
Writing	weather report; descriptive; letter writing	**Descriptive writing** Remind the children of the work they have done on fact and opinion. A report is strictly factual whereas a letter can contain the opinions of the writer. **Pcm 1** – Descriptive writing, gives the children practice in sequencing and describing windy weather conditions.
Working with words	choosing the right words	Encourage the children to use the terminology introduced in the Beaufort Scale. The children can choose three of the words and write about how they would feel being out in such a wind.

Answers

Comprehension

1. When there is a strong breeze you can see large branches move.
2. The wind is travelling at over 117 kph/73 mph when there is a hurricane blowing.
3. When you can see twigs breaking off, the type of wind is a gale.
4. When the wind is travelling at 30 – 39 kph it is Force 5.

Working with words

2. hurricane = a violent, windy storm.
   breeze = a gentle wind.
   gale = a very strong wind but less than a hurricane or tempest.
   typhoon = a violent storm in the China seas.
   tempest = violent storm of wind, often with rain or snow.
   mistral = cold North West wind in Mediterranean parts of France.
   tornado = violent storm, especially in West Africa and the United States.

See also: **p.37**, **Skills** notes.

Nelson English — Development Book 3, Unit 5, Pcm 1

name _____ date _____

Descriptive writing

Number the pictures in the right order.

Write a description of what is happening in each picture.
Remember to describe what the weather is like.

Development Unit 6

Development Book Aims:

1 Research skills.

2 Persuasive writing.

India

Teaching notes		
Stimulus	encyclopedia entries; travel brochure; photographs	*The Macmillan Encyclopedia* entry on India. Travel brochure descriptions of India, with photographs. Photograph and information on the Taj Mahal.
Comprehension	literal – atlas, info. books, dictionary, encyclopedia; literal – travel brochure; looking at persuasive writing	**Using an encyclopedia** During this exercise children use various sources to gain information – encyclopedia, dictionary, atlas. It is essential that children research the names of India's neighbours in atlases as the encyclopedia entry and artwork map are not intended to be the only sources of information for **Comprehension** question 1. Divide the class into 7 groups, each group taking one of the countries on India's borders. They can use encyclopedias to make notes and report back to the class what they have found out.
Writing	travel brochure articles; persuasive/ dissuasive	**Writing to persuade** Discuss the differences between the encyclopedia account of India and that found in the travel brochure extracts. **Pcm 1** – Writing to persuade, will support the children when looking for the language of persuasion. **Visit the Taj Mahal** Discuss the photograph and make a class list of adjectives to describe it before the children write. The children could also write travel brochure excerpts for special places in their locality. These could be compiled into a local guide book. **Writing to dissuade** The best starting point for this exercise is a discussion about a place where the children would not like to go.
Working with words	phrases to persuade/ dissuade	Children can read out their sentences so that others can say whether they would be persuaded or dissuaded.

Answers

Comprehension

1 Pakistan, Afghanistan, China, Nepal, Bhutan, Burma, Bangladesh.

2 population = number of people in the country.
dialects = the languages of a particular district.
pulses = peas, beans, lentils, etc.
jute = glossy fibre made from plants, used for making sacks and strong string.
industries = businesses that make goods.

1 Bharat.
2 The language of a particular district.
3 Rice, pulses and cereals.
4 West.
5 Wheat, rice.

See also: **p.40**, **Skills** notes.

Nelson English — Development Book 3, Unit 6, Pcm 1

name _____ date _____

Writing to persuade

Read Kim's description of her holiday.

> I went to the seaside for my holiday. It was a lovely place. The beach was clean and there were miles and miles of soft sand. I found some really interesting rockpools with crabs and other small creatures. I paddled in the warm sea and sunbathed as it was wonderfully hot.
>
> In the evening I went to the amusements. Some of the games were really exciting and the flashing lights and the music were great.

Underline the words and phrases that would persuade you to visit this beach.

Use the words and phrases in sentences of your own.

_____
_____
_____
_____
_____
_____
_____
_____
_____
_____

Published by Thomas Nelson and Sons Ltd 1995

Nelson English © John Jackman and Wendy Wren 1995.

Development Unit 7

Development Book Aims:

1. To introduce personal writing in the form of autobiography as an extension to the diary form.

An Indian childhood

Teaching notes

Stimulus	autobiography; time lines; pictures	Narrative text by Madhur Jaffrey: *The days of the banyan tree.* Time lines.
Comprehension	literal – text	**Autobiographies** The narrative text introduces the children to an author writing about her personal experiences. **Writing about yourself** Discuss Deepak's and Gemma's time lines with the children. What other information can they think of that would be appropriate?
Writing	time line; personal/ autobiography; letter writing	**Pcm 1** – Personal details, can be given as homework so that the children have the necessary information to make their own time line and tackle the **Working with words** section at the end of the unit. The school register is also useful in this context for dates of birth, starting school, etc. Discuss an event common to all the children e.g. a school trip, a Christmas concert, etc., before they write about something that happened only to them. **Writing letters** The 'things to think about' will help the children to structure their letter. See **Skills Book 3**, page 32 to remind the children of how to set out a personal letter.
Working with words	personal details	The children can use the information from their **pcm** in this section. Discuss occasions when they may have to provide their personal details, and show them a passport. They can design their own passports.

Answers

Comprehension

1. The banyan tree was so big and its branches took root again so it looked like many trees.

2. The imaginary home of the dead, of ghosts and goblins.

3. 'a blessed tree because it provided so much shade'; 'the burning months of May and June'; 'scorching winds'; 'sky overhead felt like an oven with its door left open'.

4. She was afraid of bumping into a ghost.

See also: **p.43**, **Skills** notes.

name _____ date _____

Personal details

First name(s)	
Family name	
Address	
Telephone number	
Age	
Height	
Weight	
Shoe size	
Colour of hair	
Colour of eyes	

Add other personal details below.

Development Unit 8

Development Book Aims:

1. To continue work on writing instructions.

2. To give the children further practice in writing notes.

3. To provide the opportunity for simple poetry writing.

Remember, remember the 5th of November

Teaching notes

Stimulus	poetry; acrostics; instructions; pictures	Modern poetry: *Fireworks* by James Reeves, to introduce the context of fireworks.
Comprehension	literal – poetry; inferential – poetry	The comprehension questions concentrate on the use of descriptive language.
Writing	acrostics; shape poetry; analysing instructions; posters; research – encyclopedia and info. books; making notes	**Acrostic poetry** Children can choose other names of fireworks to write their poems about or they can make up appropriate names. Discuss the names of fireworks with the children to make them appreciate that the name reflects the effect of the firework in the sense of what it looks like or the sound it makes. **Shape poetry** The example given of shape poetry uses words connected with a particular thing, i.e. a bonfire. Some shape poetry repeats the same word. Tackle this as a class discussion first. Ask for suggestions of something connected with Bonfire Night and compile a list on the board of suitable words for the shape poem, e.g. fireworks – fizzing, exploding, colourful, sparkling, whizzing, banging, crackling, etc. **Writing instructions** Children have been asked before to write instructions for performing a simple task, in **Development Book 2**. Here they are required to look at written instructions and analyse the reasoning behind them. The task also looks at the way instructions are presented so that they will be followed. The children are to design a poster to make one or two of the instructions visually powerful. Encourage them to plan the poster in their books first and then do the final artwork on large sheets of paper for display. This is a good opportunity to discuss the pros and cons of celebrating Bonfire Night. Do the children think it is a good idea? Do they have fireworks at home or do they go to an organised display? Which is better? This kind of discussion is a good preparation for the work in Unit 12 which looks at persuasive writing in the form of pros and cons for various topics. **Making notes** The children need to use simple information retrieval skills by looking at encyclopedias and reference books. **Pcm 1** – Making notes, will give them a structure for their work and introduces the idea of questions as a basis for making notes.
Working with words	similes	What other common similes do the children know? Compile a class list on the board.

Answers

Comprehension

1. 'like sudden fiery flowers'.
   'like buds too wonderful to name'.
   'like whirling marigolds'.

2. 'like whirling marigolds'.

3. Sight

4. (Individual answers.)

See also: **p.45**, **Skills** notes.

name _____ date _____

Making notes

When you are making notes it helps to think of the questions you would like answered.

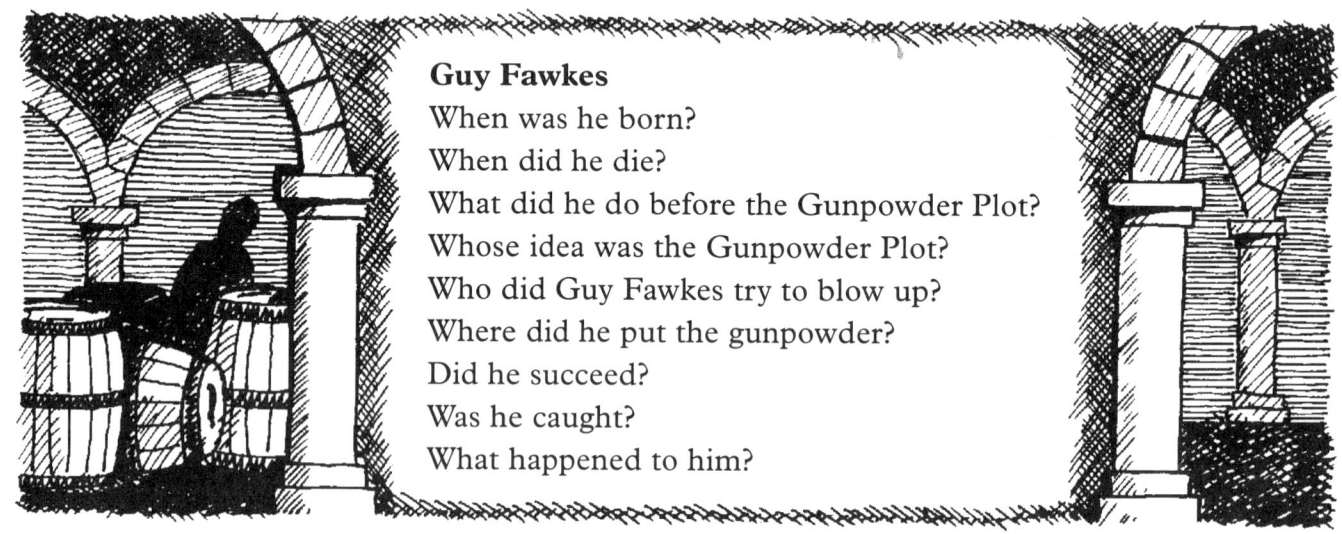

Guy Fawkes
When was he born?
When did he die?
What did he do before the Gunpowder Plot?
Whose idea was the Gunpowder Plot?
Who did Guy Fawkes try to blow up?
Where did he put the gunpowder?
Did he succeed?
Was he caught?
What happened to him?

Find the answers to the questions.
Use the answers to write about Guy Fawkes.

Development Unit 9

Development Book Aims:

1 To look at story endings.

2 To continue work on descriptive writing.

Bushfire

Teaching notes

Stimulus	narrative text; info. on story endings; pictures; rock painting	**Bushfire** A narrative extract from *Wildfire* by Mavis Thorpe Clark.

Comprehension	literal – narrative; inferential – narrative; literal – picture; inferential – picture	The comprehension is in the form of 'True or false' questions, requiring the children to interpret the passage both literally and inferentially.
		    Discuss with the children how they would feel in the same situation.
		Story endings
		As part of the initial planning for narrative writing, children must know how their story is going to end before they begin writing. This exercise highlights the intended effect on the reader. Discuss other books the children have read, ask them to recount the ending and say how it made them feel. They could work in groups and find three stories that fit into each of the categories, i.e.
		    happy-ever-after stories;
		    stories which evoke fear and excitement;
		    sad stories;
		    stories with an unexpected ending.
		Which do they like best?

Writing	planning a story – endings; finishing the story; descriptive; list of adjectives and adverbs	**Picture study**
		The children are encouraged to choose vocabulary that will give an effective description. Again this work is connected with how the reader is meant to feel.
		    Choose other pictures for oral description.
		    Go back to the initial passage *Bushfire* and ask the children to pick out the adjectives. What do they think would be the effect if the story had been written without the adjectives?

Working with words	*fire* words	Dictionary work to extend vocabulary. Can the children find any more fire words?

Answers

Comprehension

1 False. ('Bill knew the way so well that he went forward unerringly.')

2 True. ('Jan was coo-eeing. It did not sound very loud;')

3 False. ('She was crying, and so distraught that she didn't ask how or why they were there.')

4 True. ('a fierce gust had arisen again, and fire was spotting over their heads … as though the fire had suddenly found its mark, and was aiming with accuracy.')

5 False. ('retreat was cut off.')

See also: **p.48**, **Skills** notes.

Development Unit 10

Development Book Aims:

1. To use comparative situations as a stimulus for descriptive writing.
2. To give the opportunity to write from personal experience.

Victorian schooldays

Teaching notes

Stimulus	photographs; narrative text – classic fiction; pictures	Victorian class photograph: Cambo school, Northumberland c.1890. Modern school photograph. Narrative extract from *Hard Times* by Charles Dickens.
Comprehension	literal – photos; inferential – text	**Victorian schooldays** The picture stimulus provides a contrast to stimulate writing. The work can be extended by discussing the actual school building. Some children will be in a modern school while others may well be in a Victorian building. The initial work on compiling lists can be done as a group activity. *Hard Times* This passage introduces some quite sophisticated concepts regarding exactly what education should be about. The comprehension questions should be tackled orally first, in either a class or group situation.
Writing	making notes; descriptive; personal – expressing preferences; personal/ autobiography	**Writing about your own experience** Can the children remember any unusual occurrence on their first day at school? Did it turn out as they imagined or was it completely different? Have any of the children changed school? How did they feel about joining a class where everyone else knew each other? **Pcm 1** – Writing about your own experience, will help the children to structure their work.
Working with words	*quad* words; *bi* words; *tri* words	Follow up this work with *pent-*, *hex-*, *oct-*, and *dec-* words.

Answers

Comprehension – Victorian schooldays

1. **different:** size of classroom; numbers of pupils; arrangement of desks/tables, with Victorian children crowded close together in desks and today's children seated freely around tables; formal Victorian pose compared with relaxed, unbothered modern photo; very tidy room then, rather cluttered room now; severe clothes then, unlike now; big central lamp and desks in front of windows then, but electric light allows modern schoolrooms to be more easily lit up.
   same: use of walls to pin up charts; teachers standing, active, and pupils seated, working.

Comprehension – *Hard Times*

1. (Individual answers.)
2. Answers which suggest that the school was impersonal, not friendly.
3. Answers to suggest that while Bitzer's answer was factually correct he had not mentioned anything about the beauty of the animal or anything to do with a person's emotional response to it.
4. (Individual answers.)
5. Answers to suggest that while facts are important they do not always provide a full answer.

Working with words

1. quadrangle = a four-sided figure, a rectangle; a four-sided space surrounded by buildings.
   quadrilateral = any four-sided figure.
   quadrille = a square dance for four people; a piece of music for such a dance.

2. biped = a creature with two legs.
   bifocal = glasses that can focus on things near at hand and at a distance.
   bilingual = speaking or writing in two languages.

3. tricycle = a cycle with three wheels.
   trio = a group of three.
   triplets = three children born at the same time to the same mother.

See also: **p.51–55, Skills** notes.

Writing about your own experience

Answer these questions about your first day at school.

Were you looking forward to going to school?

_____

Were you afraid of going to school?

_____

How did you travel to school?

_____

Did you know any of the other children?

_____

What was your teacher called?

_____

What sorts of things did you do on your first day?

_____

What did you do for lunch? Packed lunch, school dinner, go home?

_____

How did you feel after your first day at school?

_____

Use the answers to the questions to write about your first day at school. Use the back of this worksheet if you need more space.

_____
_____
_____
_____
_____
_____

Development Unit 11

Development Book Aims:

1 To analyse different types of writing with regard to purpose and audience.

Forests

Teaching notes

Stimulus	narrative text; annotated diagram; info. on purpose and audience; pictures	Narrative extract from *The Lord of the Rings* by J R R Tolkien.
Comprehension	literal – text; inferential – text; literal – diagram; inferential – diagram	The comprehension questions lead the children into looking at how they respond to the passage. Encourage the use of the illustration to help the children appreciate the atmosphere the author is trying to create. To emphasise the need for carefully chosen vocabulary, the children could write a description of a ride through a forest which was cheerful and enjoyable. **Learning about forests** This is a very different type of writing on the same topic. The comprehension is literal in nature and deals with facts rather than reader response. When the children have worked through the rest of the unit, go back to the two initial stimuli and discuss the purpose of each and who the children think is the intended audience.
Writing	analysing types of writing – purpose/ audience; classifying types of writing	**Purpose and audience** After the children have read the examples in each of the categories under **What type of writing is it?**, class/group work could: 1 add more types of writing to each category; 2 give an example of each type of writing, e.g. stories – *The Five Children and It*. Can the children think of any more examples both for themselves as the audience and for other people as the audience? **Pcm 1** – Who is the audience? gives practice in identifying the audience for different types of writing. This can be repeated with a selection of books from the library.
Working with words	opposites with *dis*	Can the children find any more words that make their opposites with *dis*? e.g. courteous, hearten, honest, infect, loyal, obedient, please, etc.

Answers

Comprehension – *The Lord of the Rings*

1 Answers:
writhing and interlacing roots;
no undergrowth;
ground was rising steadily;
trees became taller, darker and thicker;
no sound;
occasional drip of moisture;
still leaves;
abominable wood.

2 (Individual answers.)

3 (Individual answers.)

4 The wood was very unpleasant and threatening.

5 keeping away from = avoiding.
happening now and then = occasional.
speaking in a soft, low voice = whispering.

Comprehension – learning about forests

1 The top layer of the forest is called the canopy.

2 The sun is important for trees because they need energy from the sun to grow.

3 The forest is dark underneath the canopy. There are trunks of the largest trees, smaller trees and shrubs.

4 The shrub layer is on the floor of the forest.

5 The ground layer is where you would find mosses and insect life.

6 (Individual answers suggesting that it is impossible to tell the writer's feelings.)

Writing – purpose and audience

Writing for myself:
shopping lists, telephone messages, poems, menus, diaries, notes, stories.

Writing for people I know:
letters, menus, instructions, stories, shopping lists, adverts, poems, reports, telephone messages, notes, maps.

Writing for people I don't know:
letters, menus, instructions, stories, speeches, newspaper articles, adverts, poems, reports, notes, plays, maps.

Working with words

disagree = to quarrel.
discontent = unhappy, not satisfied.
disembark = to go ashore from a ship.
dislike = to not like, to hate.
disobey = not to obey.

See also: **p.56–61**, Skills notes.

Nelson English — Development Book 3, Unit 11, Pcm 1

name _____ date _____

Who is the audience?

Who do you think would read these books?
Match the audience with the book.

Books shown:
- LEARNING TO SKI
- Cooking Italian Food
- Road maps of Scotland
- RAILWAY TIMETABLE
- How to look after your dog
- UFOs. Do they exist?

Audience list:
- someone going skiing
- a dog owner
- someone interested in aliens
- someone interested in Italian food
- someone travelling by car in Scotland
- someone who travels by train

Book title	Audience

Published by Thomas Nelson and Sons Ltd 1995   Nelson English © John Jackman and Wendy Wren 1995.

Development Unit 12

Development Book Aims:

1. To introduce the idea of the *theme* of a piece of writing.
2. Work on characters with regard to thoughts and feelings.
3. More work on persuasive writing.

Eat to live

Teaching notes

Stimulus	factual text; poetry; info. on persuasive writing; pictures	**Reynard the Fox** Extract from the traditional verse *Reynard the Fox* by John Masefield. **I Saw a Jolly Hunter** Just as the two pieces of writing on the forest in the previous unit dealt with the same topic in very different ways, so this modern poem by Charles Causley provides a contrast to *Reynard the Fox*.
Comprehension	literal – poetry; inferential – poetry	**Reynard the Fox** The comprehension questions ask children to read between the lines and also to consider what effect the poet intended to have on the reader. Discuss the description of the fox throughout the chase. How does that description make the children feel? Do they want the fox to be caught or escape? **I Saw a Jolly Hunter** The comprehension questions lead the children to consider that while the theme is the same and the reader is intended to feel the same, the way the two poems are written is very different. Discuss how both poets make the reader feel. John Masefield makes the reader feel horrified, while Charles Causley makes his point by making us laugh.
Writing	imaginative – feelings; pros and cons	**Writing about feelings** In **Development Book 2** work on characters was introduced with regard to physical description and characteristics. Here the work is developed to include their thoughts and feelings. This ties in with how a writer wants the reader to respond to a particular character. Understanding how desperate Reynard felt while being chased helps the reader to feel sympathy with the fox. Discuss the various other possibilities with the children, e.g. Reynard could be not worried at all as he has often outrun the dogs. He could enjoy the chase and go the long way home to tire the dogs out. He could treat it as a game and play 'hide and seek' with the dogs, feeling that he is much cleverer and can outwit them any day. **Writing to persuade** The children would benefit from an initial class discussion followed by group work. Each group could report back to the class. If the children have grasped the idea, this work could be extended into a debate.
Working with words	idioms	The class can make a collection of idioms for display.

Answers

Comprehension – *Reynard the Fox*

1. The things that would help the fox to survive were that he was strong, could run fast and was cunning.
2. (Individual answers.)
3. (Individual answers.)
4. The fox willed himself to go on and escape; he would not be defeated.
5. The poet wants the reader to be on the fox's side. You can tell this because he describes in detail how awful it would be for the fox if he were caught. The reader is made to feel sympathetic towards the fox.

Comprehension – *I Saw a Jolly Hunter*

1. The theme of both poems is hunting animals for sport.
2. Yes.
3. The poets feel that hunting animals for sport is wrong.
4. They want you to agree with them.

Working with words

Once in a blue moon = very infrequently.

Stick to your guns = you will not be dissuaded, you are very determined.

A bolt from the blue = a surprise.

Over the moon = very happy about something.

See also: **p.62**, **Skills** notes.

Development Unit 13

Development Book Aims:

1 To continue work on basic research techniques.

2 To work on planning and writing up interviews.

Printing and writing

Teaching notes

Stimulus	factual text; pictures; fact file; info. on biographies	**Printing and writing** A brief factual account of the written and printed forms of communication. Find out what the children already know about the subject before reading the account.
Comprehension	literal – text; inferential – text	**Printing and writing** The comprehension questions ask the children to draw on their own experiences and also to analyse the passage in terms of purpose and audience.
Writing	research – encyclopedia, info. books; interviews – note-taking	**Research** In previous units the children have been introduced to dictionaries, encyclopedias and simple reference books as sources of information. They can now draw on these skills to research William Caxton. The task can be prepared by a class discussion, compiling a list of questions the children need to find the answers to, or it can be used to assess how efficient they are at research skills on an individual basis. **Interviews** Continuing the work on finding information, this section takes the children through the process of interviewing. **Pcm 1** – Interviews, gives the children a structure for their work but they should be encouraged to think of their own questions as well. This can be extended into a drama activity. The questions are prepared and then the interview takes place with an audience.
Working with words	writers	This section can be extended by asking the children if they know or can find out what the following people write: journalist; biographer; copy writer; script writer.

Answers

Comprehension

1 Both printing and writing communicate meaning but we can print something over and over again without having to write it out every time.

2 (Individual answers.)

3 (Individual answers.)

4 The purpose of the piece of writing about printing and writing is to communicate information.

5 The audience is anyone interested in the subject.

Working with words

stories
= novelists, story writers, authors

poetry
= poets

plays
= playwrights

history books
= historians

See also: **p.64**, **Skills** notes.

Nelson English — DEVELOPMENT BOOK 3 — **Unit 13** — Pcm 1

name _____   date _____

Interviews

Choose a person in your class.
Ask them these questions.
Write down the answers.

What is your name?	
How old are you?	
Where were you born?	
Have you any brothers and sisters?	
Have you ever moved house?	
What do you do in your spare time?	
What do you want to do when you leave school?	

Use your notes to write up the interview as a playscript or as a factual piece of writing. Use the back of this worksheet if you need more space.

_____
_____
_____
_____
_____
_____
_____
_____
_____
_____

Published by Thomas Nelson and Sons Ltd 1995   Nelson English © John Jackman and Wendy Wren 1995.

Development Unit 13a

Development Book Aims:

1 To introduce newspaper articles.

Read all about it!

Teaching notes

Stimulus	newspaper report; map; photograph; picture	**Read all about it!** Text and map from *The Times* newspaper about the October 1987 gales.
Comprehension	literal – report; literal – map; inferential – photograph	**Read all about it!** Discuss the extracts from the newspaper in terms of fact and opinion: what actually happened, what are the journalists expressing an opinion about? Discuss the reasons for including the map. Is it useful? Is it a good way of presenting the information? **Danger at sea** Why do newspapers use photographs? What do the children think and feel when they look at the photograph? Who has the journalist interviewed for part of this report on the gale at sea? In this introduction to newspapers the children need to appreciate that the visual content of each page is as important as the words. Newspapers are read quickly and need to present information in a way that is easily understood. Choose articles from other newspapers and let the children discuss them in groups with regard to the layout of text, pictures, maps, etc. The language, headlines, advertisements, etc. will be features in **Development Books 4 and 5**.
Writing	newspaper reports – facts; eye-witness accounts	**Writing a newspaper report** Children have to concentrate on the facts of the incident and on eye-witness accounts. **Pcm 1** – Writing a newspaper report, will give them further practice. This work can be extended by using an incident from a story book which has to be written up as a newspaper report.
Working with words	abbreviations	Children can find other abbreviations in the dictionary and make a list for a friend to work on. How quickly can they find the answers?

Answers

Comprehension – *Read all about it!* text

1 People would have been out of doors and, therefore, more people would have been injured.

2 The wind was blowing from the south and the south west.

3 A 'minor road' is a small road, not a motorway or dual carriageway.

4 A great many trees had been blown down.

Comprehension – *Read all about it!* map

1 Hurricane Force 12 (73 mph and over).

2 At 7 am in London the wind speed was 94 mph.

3 The wind was blowing at 134 mph in Point du Roc.

4 The oil rig that broke away from its moorings was in Viking Field, in the North Sea.

Working with words

adj = adjective
cm = centimetre
cert = certified, certificate, certificated. ('Cert' – for 'certainty' – is also typically said of a horse that is expected to win a race!)
MP = Member of Parliament, Military Police
Dr = Doctor, Drive
RSPCA = Royal Society for the Prevention of Cruelty to Animals
GB = Great Britain
Ave = Avenue

See also: **p.64**, **Skills** notes. 103

Nelson DEVELOPMENT BOOK 3
Unit 13a
ENGLISH **Pcm 1**

name _____ date _____

Writing a newspaper report

Here is a list of facts about a flood in Castle Village.

- heavy rain
- people taken out of the village by fire brigade
- cars stranded
- nearby river bursts banks
- house flooded
- water down main street
- Mrs Brown, who had water running through the house, interviewed by local newspaper reporter.

Use the facts to write the newspaper report.
What will you call your newspaper report?
What do you think Mrs Brown said to the reporter?

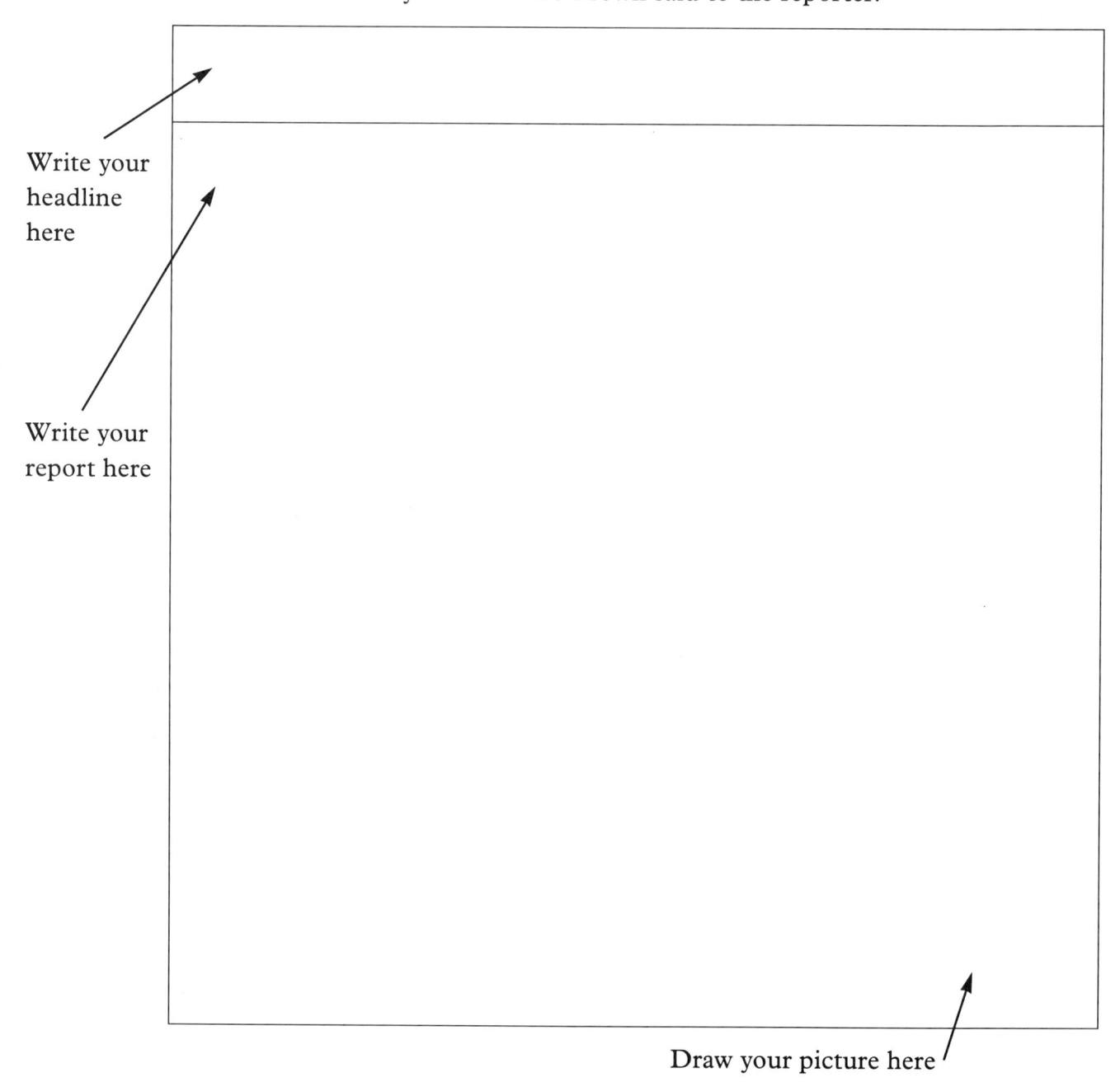

Write your headline here

Write your report here

Draw your picture here

Published by Thomas Nelson and Sons Ltd 1995   Nelson English © John Jackman and Wendy Wren 1995.

Development Unit 14

Development Book Aims:

1. To give the opportunity for comparing and contrasting different accounts and interpretations of the same event.

2. To continue work on purpose and audience within a specific context.

Earth ... In the beginning

Teaching notes		
Stimulus	narrative – biblical text; narrative – legend; presenting information; pictures	The story of creation from the Bible. The Egyptian creation story.
Comprehension	literal – biblical text; literal – legend	Most children will be familiar with the biblical account of creation. The Egyptian story is another interpretation. Do the children know any others? There may be children in the class of different religious persuasions and it is important to investigate these cultures with regard to traditional stories of creation. The comprehension questions will highlight important similarities in the stories and can lead to a discussion of why so many cultures have accounts of creation.
Writing	purpose and audience – writing for young children; research – dictionary	**Presenting information** This task lends itself to pair/group work. The children can interview pupils from a younger class to find out what sorts of thing they like in books. Through class discussion prepare a list of questions about pictures, colour, size of print, number of words on a page, etc. The children can use this research when they are making their books. **Pcm 1** – Presenting information will support some children in structuring their work. It is likely that most children will choose the biblical story to work on as this is most familiar. Try to encourage some pairs/groups to tackle the Egyptian story.
Working with words	complex/ simple words	This can be used as part of the preparation for writing the story for younger children. See **Skills Book** 3 Unit 14 for work on the thesaurus.

Answers

Comprehension

1. Bible – God; Egyptian creation story – Ra. Each is an all-powerful figure in the creation stories but they differ because God named things and they were immediately created whereas Ra created other gods too when he named things, and then made himself the first Pharaoh of Egypt and ruled for thousands of years.

2. They both created things by speaking.

3. light
sky
land
sea
plants: flowers, grass, trees, grain
living things: fish, birds, insects, animals
man

4. sun
wind
rain
earth
sky
river Nile
all the things that are upon the earth
mankind

5. (Individual answers suggesting that the lists are very similar and differ only slightly in the order in which things were created.)

Working with words

roam = wander, walk about
explode = bang, blow up, blow to pieces
soar = fly, glide

See also: p.67–74, **Skills** notes.

Presenting information

Here are the pictures in a young child's book about the creation.
Write what is happening so a young child can read it.

Quiz Answers
Skills Track Unit 2:
Be your own weather forecaster

Cumulonimbus

There are 175 words that can be made from this one: how many of the following have your class found?

B: bill, bin, bloc, blinis, bliss, blobs, blooms, blossoms, bobs, boils, bolls, bolus, bombs, bonbons, bonus, boom, boon, bosom, boss, bosun, bucolic, bulb, bull, bullion, bunion, buns, bus

C: climbs, clinic, club, cob, cocoon, coil, coins, col, colon, colossus, column, comb, combo, comic, common, communion, cons, concuss, conscious, consul, cool, cos, cosmic, cosmos, council, couscous, cousins, cubs, culls, cumin, cumulus, cuss

I: icon, ill, illusion, inn, innocuous, insulin, ion, ionic

L: lib., limbo, limbs, lino., lion, lissom, lobs, loci, loco., locum, locus, loins, lolls, loo, loom, lop, loss, lull, luminous

M: millions, mill, mimic, mini, minibus, minim, minimum, minion, minus, miss, mission, mo, mob, moll, mollusc, mono, monsoon, moo, moon, moss, Ms, mucous, mucus, mullion, mull, music, mum, Muslim, muslin

N: nib, nil, nisi, no, nob, nonunion, noon, nouns, nub, null, numb, nun, nuncio

O: oil, ominous, omnibus, on, onion, onus, osmosis

S: scion, scullion, sculls, scum, sic, silicon, silicosis, silo, sill, sins, sinuous, sinus, slim, slob, slum, snob, snub, sobs, soil, so, sol, solo, son, sonic, soon, sos, so–so, soul, subconscious, sub, succumbs, summons, sumo, sums, sun

U: unconscious, union, unionism, unison, us

Nelson English Skills Book 3
Record of Progress

Name:

Unit completed/date	1 Winter weather	2 Be your own weather forecaster	3 King James	4 Tudor and Stuart pastimes	5 Wings	6 The Ganges – a holy river	7 How Mowgli joined the wolves	8 Fire beneath our feet	9 Fire!	10 Victorian homes	10a Victorian fashion	11 Travelling the River Amazon	11a Caves and underground rivers	12 Fascinating body facts	13 Newspapers	14 Moon – in the future	14a Earth	Comments
comprehension	4	8	12	16	22	26	30	34	38	44	48	54	58	62	66	70	74	
vocabulary enrichment	5						31	35			50						75	
vocabulary choices		9			23		33	36	41	47	51		61	65	68			
nouns/pronouns			11	17	25						57					73	77	
plurals	7		10	19	29					45								
verbs		11	15															
tenses				18		32							60					
adjectives/adverbs	7							37				50		60	65			
subject/predicate				18				36										
sentences													57	64		72	76	
direct speech						24			40	46				56				
punctuation	6	10	14		24		37								68			
conjunctions																		
paragraphs							32		40							71		
prefixes/suffixes		13																
letters																		
dictionary/thesaurus						28												
possessive nouns																		
tch pattern		11	15															
silent letters			15					36										
ear pattern					19													
soft c					25		29											
i before e			13				33											
ure pattern										41	47							
are pattern																		
able/ible pattern																		
tion pattern											51			61				
ness pattern															65			
age/dge pattern																	77	
le/el/al pattern															69			
ght pattern																	73	

Key
28 activity undertaken
28 activity undertaken and understood
28 activity revisited and understood

108

Nelson English
Development Book 3
Record of Progress

Name:

Unit completed/date	1 A Winter's tale	2 Footprints in the snow	3 Tudor and Stuart theatre	4 Tudor and Stuart beliefs	5 Gale warning!	6 India	7 An Indian childhood	8 Remember, remember...	9 Bushfire	10 Victorian schooldays	11 Forests	12 Eat to live	13 Printing and writing	13a Read all about it!	14 Earth...In the beginning	Comments
literal comprehension	10	14	20		30	36	46		54	58	60	68	72	76		
inferential comprehension	10	14	20		36		50	52	54	58	60	68	72			
picture comprehension	4			21	24							65				
imaginative writing	4															
descriptive writing		12	22		28			51	53							
personal writing		12				38			56							
factual writing					27							69				
using a dictionary		13	19	23	29	30		51	57	63			73	75		
map reading						30										
personal letters					28	40										
analysing	6						48									
drawing diagrams						39		48								
narrative writing	5								48					80		
instructions							44									
note-taking							45									
plays			16	22												
poetry comprehension				23			42									
using charts/diagrams					26					32		64 66	67			
writing to persuade						32										
writing to dissuade					35											
poetry writing						43										
purpose and audience										62					80	
interviews																
newspaper reports												70	75			
using a thesaurus															80	

Key
[28 shaded] activity undertaken
[28 crossed] activity undertaken and understood
[28 double-crossed] activity revisited and understood

Thomas Nelson & Sons Ltd
Nelson House Mayfield Road
Walton-on-Thames Surrey
KT12 5PL UK

Thomas Nelson Australia
102 Dodds Street
South Melbourne
Victoria 3205 Australia

Nelson Canada
1120 Birchmont Road
Scarborough Ontario
M1K 5G4 Canada

© John Jackman, Wendy Wren 1994, 1995

First edition published by
Thomas Nelson and Sons Ltd 1994

Revised edition published by
Thomas Nelson and Sons Ltd 1995

I(T)P   Thomas Nelson is an
         International Thomson Publishing Company
I(T)P   is used under licence

ISBN 0-17-424606-4
NPN 9 8 7 6 5

All rights reserved. No paragraph of this publication may be reproduced, copied or transmitted save with written permission or in accordance with the provisions of the Copyright, Design and Patents Act 1988, or under the terms of any licence permitting limited copying issued by the Copyright Licensing Agency,
90 Tottenham Court Road,
London, W1P 9HE.

The publisher grants permission for copies of photocopy master pages only to be made without fee as follows:

Private purchasers may make copies for their own use or for use by their own students; school purchasers may make copies for use by the staff and students within and of the institution only. This permission to copy does not extend to additional institutions or branches of an institution, which should purchase a separate master copy of the book for their own use.

For copying in any other circumstances prior permission must be obtained in writing from Thomas Nelson and Sons Ltd.

Printed in China

Acknowledgements

The authors and publisher are grateful for permission to include the following copyright material:

> The Kellogg Company of Great Britain for the use of its registered trademark *Rice Krispies* and associated intellectual property rights.
>
> *It sings* © Aileen Fisher, from **East of the Sun** published by Hodder and Stoughton.
>
> Pages 32 and 99 of *The Nelson Concise Thesaurus* © Gordon Pemberton.

The authors and publisher would like to thank the staff and pupils of the following schools, who have generously given their time to trial Nelson English. Their comments and criticisms have helped develop and polish the early concepts.

Ayr Grammar Primary School, Ayr
Beeston Primary School, Leeds
Caversham Primary School, Caversham, Reading
Cramond School, Cramond, Edinburgh
Fairfield Primary School, Basingstoke
Hampton Hill Junior School, Hampton Hill, Middlesex
Hampton Infants' School, Hampton, Middlesex
Holt Primary, Holt, Clwyd
Horndean Junior School, Hampshire
Lambton Primary School, Washington, Co. Durham
Laurel Bank School, Glasgow
Marlborough JMI School, Isleworth, Middlesex
Old Fleet Primary, Hull
St. Nicholas RC Combined School, Exeter
The Bocombra Primary School, Portadown,
Co. Armagh

We should also like to acknowledge the valuable advice and guidance received from our consultants:

Gervase Phinn, Senior General Inspector for English, North Yorkshire County Council
Patricia Gordon, Craigie College, University of Paisley

and from our teacher advisers:

Bill Ball, Maureen Barlin, Penny Bridgeland,
Hilary Frost, Hilary Harriman, Roye Jackman,
Sarah Lindsay, Isobel McGhee, Richard Painter,
Mary Pereira, Liz Purvis, Pat Ranson, Andrea Samuels,
Penny Seal, Eve Stephens and Tony D. Triggs.

The authors and publishers gratefully acknowledge the valuable contribution of the following documents:

National Curriculum (1995) England and Wales.

National Guidelines (Scotland) English Language 5 – 14.

Curriculum (Programmes of Study and Attainment Targets in English) Order (Northern Ireland) 1990.